| PREFACE

Charles Edward Chapman first introduced me to the caudillo, to the personalism and variegated background characteristic of caudillos. Chapman classified them according to the quality of their services to society. He did not attempt to define them as political or social phenomena. My interest in the era of independence and the nineteenth century in northern South America has involved me with the caudillo and his reason for being. I have long been troubled by frequent references in scholarly and popular works to the caudillos as military men and by consistent presentation of caudillism as a species of militarism. It was, however, vigorous discussion over the nature and causes of caudillism while in the Bureau of Intelligence and Research of the Department of State which drove me to make the effort to formulate and verify the conclusions which I had been accumulating for some years. The resulting study began as an article in 1961 but soon overflowed such dimensions.

Long convinced of important differences in the development of the several Latin American nations, I resolved to focus on one country. Consequently, what I have to say on the subject is directed to Venezuela even though some of my definitions and conclusions may have wider adjusted application. Venezuela was chosen for a number of reasons: it lies within my area of interest; its political history has been least effectively disturbed by Church-State difficulties; and it lacks a large unassimilated Indian population. Above all, its politics constitute a classic example of the role of individualized, i.e., entrepreneurial political violence, which is an essential trait of caudillism.

The author wishes to acknowledge the generous assistance of the Ohio University Library, the Bancroft Library of the University of California, the Law Division and the Hispanic Foundation of the Library of Congress, the National Archives of the United States, the Academia Nacional de la Historia of Venezuela, and the Fundación John Boulton of Caracas. Rollie Poppino of the Davis Campus of the University of California, Elizabeth Hyman of the Division of American Republics, Bureau of Intelligence and Research of the Department of State, Stanley Stein of Princeton University, Lyle N. McAlister of the University of Florida, and Harry R. Stevens of Ohio University read and commented on the manuscript at various stages of its preparation.

ROBERT L. GILMORE

CONTENTS

POLITICAL PERIODIZATION AND PRESIDENTIAL ADMINISTRATIONS OF VENEZUELA

1810–1823 STRUGGLE FOR
VENEZUELAN
INDEPENDENCE

1819–1830 THE REPUBLIC OF
COLOMBIA

1826–1830 VENEZUELA WITHDRAWS
FROM COLOMBIA

1830–1935 THE ERA OF THE
CAUDILLO

1830–1848 PÁEZ AND THE PATRICIATE	1830–1835 *José Antonio Páez*
	1835–1839 *José María Vargas (1835–1836) Andrés Narvarte (1836–1837) Carlos Soublette (1837–1839)*
	1839–1843 *José Antonio Páez*
	1843–1847 *Carlos Soublette*
1848–1870 ANARCHIC CAUDILLISM	1847–1851 *José Tadeo Monágas*
	1851–1855 *José Gregorio Monágas*
	1855–1858 *José Tadeo Monágas*
1858 The Patriciate Rebels	1858–1859 *Julian Castro*
1859–1864 The Federal War	1859–1863 *Pedro Gual (August–September 1859) Manuel Felipe de Tovar (September 1859–May 1861)* **Pedro Gual** *(May–August 1861) José Antonio Páez (August 1861–June 1863) Juan Falcón (June–December 1863)*
	1863–1868 *Juan Falcón*
1868–1870 Blue (Conservative) Revolution	1868–1870 *José Tadeo and José Ruperto Monágas*

1870–1935 DESPOTIC
CAUDILLISM

1870–1889	Dominance of Guzmán Blanco	1870–1877	*Antonio Guzmán Blanco*
		1877–1879	*Francisco Linares Alcántara (1877–1878) José Gregorio Valera (1878–1879)*
		1879–1884	*Antonio Guzmán Blanco*
		1884–1886	*Joaquín Crespo*
		1886–1888	*Antonio Guzmán Blanco*
1889–1903	Reversion to Anarchy	1888–1890	*Juan Pablo Rojas Paúl*
		1890–1892	*Raimundo Andueza Palacio*
		1892–1898	*Joaquín Crespo*
1898–1958	Emergence and Dominance of Andinos	1898–1899	*Ignacio Andrade*
		1899–1908	*Cipriano Castro*
1908–1935	The Absolutism of Gómez	1908–	*Juan Vicente Gómez*

CAUDILLISM AND MILITARISM IN VENEZUELA, 1810–1910

1 | THE PROBLEM OF DEFINITION

Analysis of Venezuelan society and its institutions in the nineteenth century demands a distinction between caudillism and militarism. A more precise differentiation between these terms is a basic purpose of this study. Caudillism was the preëminent trait of the political system of Venezuela from 1814 to 1935. Since 1935 Venezuela has rapidly acquired all the pressure groups of a modern industrializing society. As the only one of the pressure groups possessing an effective organization in 1935, the armed forces were inevitably involved in the turbulence of a rapidly changing society. Militarism has been, therefore, a recent problem for Venezuela.

Some consideration of the general character of militarism is a necessary backdrop against which to view the Venezuelan situation. Armed forces in the modern era have usually been defenders of the order in which they thrive. Only defeat has compelled them to accept revolutionary change; and revolutionary regimes throughout the world have formed new military forces which become conservative towards any effort to change the order which gave them being. Awareness of modern militarism arose a little over a century ago in Europe when it began to be a political issue "raised in the struggles of domestic politics as a reproach to parties and institutions which unduly furthered military desires." The Romantic Era with its "sentimentalism and conviction" knew modern militarism as an aspect of its reaction against the middle-class rationalism of the Enlightenment and against the shift of the locus of social power to the middle class.[1]

The contribution of the Romantic Era to the formation of modern Western militarism was continued by the class and group imbalances of rapidly industrializing European societies whose vertiginously aggrandized rival interests constantly advanced the armed forces from the rear echelon of policy recourse nearer that of immediate selection. Concurrently, the increasing secularization of society constantly augmented and augments the role of the military in the rituals of the state. In contrast, the national guard or largely self-equipped militia was one of the means by which the bourgeoisie, even in Venezuela, defended its interests and advanced its role in society. Its origin was linked to the opening of what Robert Palmer has labelled the Age of Democratic Revolution. It ceased to be an effective, exclusively bourgeois, institution about mid-nineteenth century. The victory—in some countries the defeat—of the middle classes in mid-century closed the Romantic Era, ended the role of the national guard as a class institution, and opened the age of the mass-based professionally-led army dependent on an industrial society. In industrial societies the managerial revolution, fraternal and veterans' associations, and totalitarian political movements have been assigned some influence in promoting militarism. It may be overemphasized.[2]

Modern militarism has meant "the domination of the military man over the civilian, an undue preponderance of military demands, an emphasis on military considerations, spirit, ideals, and scales of values in the life of states. It has also meant the imposition of heavy burdens on a people for military purposes, to the neglect of welfare and culture and the waste of the nation's best manpower in unproductive army service." [3]

Militarism as strength in terms of men and money is usually associated with imperialism, i.e., the extension of territorial holdings or of political controls. Among the Latin American nations, however, the manifestations of imperialism have been very limited. Thus in Latin America much greater emphasis and importance must be attached to the fact that the modern army sees but limited use, and in the long periods of noncombat duty militarism may flourish. Moreover, among the Latin American nations the secondary role of the armed forces of a major power, the maintenance of internal order, becomes in fact their primary role. Inevitably such a role involves them more intimately in the domestic political life of their nations. At the same time military people, like the members of any other profession, resent command by the masses and tend to cherish the ideal of the autonomous military institution free of civilian intervention despite the armed forces' dependence on the socio-

economic strength of society. A major element in the prolonged existence of militarism has been the civilian mili-
tarist in high public office who has used the armed forces to
limit change, to assure group survival and security, or to
control and discipline the governed. Somewhat less obvious
has been the militarism of the lonely crowd seeking order
and security in hierarchy and comradeship or finding in it
an emotional compensation for economic and social disappointments.[4]

Manifestations of militarism in a society have indicated
that the established regime or the old order was passing,
that significant middle and even proletarian groups were
rising to economic and political power, and that the ruling
groups of the old regime were casting about for some means
to preserve their status. It has also meant that the wars for
independence in Spanish America destroyed the old basis
for the consent of the governed directed to the monarchy,
which was the foundation and the symbol of the rule of law,
i.e., of civilian institutions. The restoration of a similar level
of attachment to civilian institutions in republican Spanish
America is still in process in most of the nations which
emerged from the Spanish Empire.

II

The preceding generalizations constitute a standard against
which to judge the existence of caudillism and militarism in
nineteenth-century Venezuela. Caudillism is not in question, but the tendency to equate it with militarism in dealing with Venezuela is in question. The linking together
of the two terms is based primarily on the fact that both are
concerned with violence. The military institution is con-

cerned with the management and use of controlled violence in the service of the state according to terms laid down by the state. When the military institution veers from this role to participate in or to influence other nonmilitary agencies and functions of the state, including its leadership, then militarism exists in greater or lesser degree. Caudillism is a political process in which violence is an essential element. It is anarchic, self-generating, instinctively aspirant to the vanished role of the monarchy.

It is deceptively easy to confuse caudillism with that version of militarism known as the Praetorian State, a label properly applied to some of the Latin American nations in the nineteenth century. David C. Rapoport has described the Praetorian State as "one where private ambitions are rarely restrained by a sense of public authority or common purpose, the role of power (i.e., wealth and force) is maximized." His analysis apparently presupposes a cacical base under the authority of those "who command wealth and violence." [5] In the Praetorian State the armed forces help select and establish national leadership in a manner which well accords with Finer's description of a military dominated state as an "empirical autocracy and oligarchy." [6]

Venezuela did not fit the foregoing definition. Its residue of political practice after the destruction of the Spanish empire was infra-praetorian. The elements of state power were so disrupted that the armed forces did not escape. The decay of the political process was more rapid than the erosion of the social cohesiveness of the old ruling groups. Society developed the symptoms of caudillism. The caudillesque state did not qualify for the praetorian label because the means of force and the capacity and will to use violence for local and national purposes were too dispersed. Nor did the element of dispersion qualify Venezuela's caudillesque society for feudal classification since it lacked the vinculation to a particular property or profession of the authority to administer, of the right to judge, of the power to regulate, and of the command over men bearing arms. Venezuelan society was at once too molded by the patterns of centralized authority, its people too individualized in the use of violence and too alienated from the new institutions for the governing of society to be either praetorian or feudal.

A related problem is the definition of a military man. The professional military man is easily identifiable, but there is a fairly common notion that any man who performs in the broader range of his occupational activities one or more military functions is, therefore, a military man. It is presumed, then, that a military function asserts a dominant influence over the outlook, conduct, and goals of an individual even though its performance be episodic, or when of frequent occurrence it is still ancillary to the vocation of the person. Such a view is unacceptable. Military men could become caudillos, but only at the sacrifice of their military character. Caudillos could become military men, but only at the price of professionalization, no matter how rudimentary. If the caudillo-become-military man desired to continue his political activity it would necessarily be through the military institution. The end result would be, if he succeeded, the formation of the Praetorian State.

Some writers hold that the habitual carrying of arms essential for violence is sufficient to classify a man as military. Thus a recent work states:

The fact that not all armies were highly organized in the past, or that they need not necessarily be so, is irrelevant here. Modern armies are cohesive and hierarchical. Some armies of the past have not been cohesive but have consisted of a mere multitude of men independent of one another and maintaining little contact between themselves. Others have not been hierarchical, but almost republican in their relations to their chiefs. The Spartan host and the Cossack settlements were cohesive enough; but republican as to command. The *voortrekkers* and the American frontiersmen were neither cohesive nor hierarchical formations. In the early stages of their development some revolutionary armies . . . resemble these primitive prototypes of the modern armies. . . .[7]

On that basis a fur-trapping expedition into the Rocky Mountains at mid-nineteenth century was in some degree an army. In more modern terms the plundering violence of the gangster should justify some future study entitled *The Era of Al Capone: A Study of Militarism in the Municipality*. Definition must rest on something more than accidentals. It must also include substance and purpose of the thing defined. A fundamental point in applying the proper label to the Venezuelan scene of the past century is the fact that its caudillism was a product of profound social disorganization, while its militarism in the present century has been a stage in a rapid re-ordering or restructuring of society marked by related pressure group imbalance.

An increasing number of publications on the military and militarism in Latin America aptly point up the varied concepts of the authors. On this point Lyle N. McAlister has reviewed the several approaches to the problem of definition of militarism in Latin America.[8] Edwin Lieuwin's *Arms and Politics in Latin America,* of recent vintage, was the first major study to take on the problem of analyzing and defining the role of the Latin American armed forces in the national period; but much remains to be done. A number of articles and contributions to symposia by Magnus Mörner, Robin Humphries, Robert Alexander, Edwin Lieuwin, León Helguerra, William S. Stokes, Lt. Col. Theodore Wyckoff, General Pedro Aramburu, Victor Alba, and John J. Johnson have touched on these themes more or less directly, but in the main for the twentieth century.[9]

A basis for militarism of the pre-modern type did exist in the Spanish empire. There were similarities between the military obligations imposed on the Spanish nobility of the Middle Ages and those of the encomenderos in the Spanish colonies: that of organizing and leading a defense force in case of local emergency, and of serving as subordinate leaders of such forces in case of regional or colonial peril from invasion or rebellion.[10] The founding of a modern Spanish army at the beginning of the sixteenth century was not duplicated, however, in the colonies. Formation of more highly trained militia units took place during the reign of Charles III (1759–1788). Militia officers and enlisted men, drawn respectively from the colonial upper class and from artisans and workers, were admitted to military *fuero* [11] in matters relating to their militia training and service. Militia members vigorously sought to include their civilian concerns under military fuero, presupposing partiality of decision by the military courts. Such abuse did not, however, represent advocacy of militarism, but a quest for social and economic advantages over one's fellows based on the enjoyment of exceptional status outside the common fuero.[12]

It has long been the custom to portray Venezuela as a barracks, a description based on Bolívar's correspondence and on the reality of the Venezuelan scene during the campaigns for independence—if the barracks are not made too professional. If the label is taken to mean a society under arms, it lacked validity after 1823, but if descriptive of the predominant political role of the quasi-professional officers formed by long campaigning in the war for independence, then the label has much to be said for it. In the latter acceptance it possessed some of the substance of militarism until 1831, and more clearly so under other conditions for the years 1944–1958. It connotes also the military institution in the role of the major pressure group in a society.

In the early decades after independence the veteran officers constituted a consensus group, but not a closely organized pressure group in the modern technical sense. They were virtually unanimous on one subject. They had created the Venezuelan state, and therefore they should lead and control it.[13] This intent was more properly, however, the expression of political entrepreneurship than of militarism. The veteran Venezuelan officers possessed much of the group indiscipline and other traits of the entrepreneur of economic liberalism. In the twentieth century, in contrast, the goals of the military institution have reflected a more corporate outlook in seeking to apply to Venezuelan society the standards of the career professionals: hierarchy, discipline, and capacitation. It is militarism, not caudillism, whose appearance and definition may be linked to the rise of the middle class, to the bureaucratization of government, to centralization of administrative authority, and to industrialization. It is associated with the disintegration of the old and the rise of a new order endangering the continued authority of the established ruling groups. This state of things did not begin to come into being in Venezuela until a century after the achievement of independence.

As a label, militarism ill comports with the personalism of nineteenth-century Venezuelan society with its accessory traits of violence, nepotism, extended families, oligarchy, and pre-industrial economy. Personalism signifies the control and exploitation of the political units serving society by individuals and by extended family groups. Its major role in a political system may indicate a specific stage of development or of decay in a given society. It has flourished among one-time colonies after the end of external controls over colonial interest groups which, freed of outside regulations, tend to dissolve in anarchic rivalry. The removal of imperial officials has usually not been accompanied by effective concordance between the continuing structure of colonial society and the political institutions adopted in the new nations.

Persistent application of the militarism label to Venezuela implies also the practice of automatic assignment of military career status and standards to any individual accorded a military title. It presumes a constant effort to impose a military regimen on Venezuelan society—an effort which has yet to be made in Venezuela. Such characterization of Venezuelan political development has been fostered by Venezuelan officials, and reformers have long blamed the military for delayed realization of representative democratic government. The term has been given some validity by active intervention of the professional armed forces in the leadership of the state since 1944. Institutionalization of violence in the political process has made the military a synonym for violence, since the actors in violence dignified their conduct with military titles and forms.

Venezuelan political history from 1830 to 1935 was notable for a descent into anarchy followed by authoritarian government. The Venezuelan patriciate or bourgeoisie—the old colonial oligarchy—attempted after the end of the war for independence to establish firmly its control over Venezuelan society. Its chosen instrument was a popular general of the war for independence who completely identified himself with the patriciate and its militia. This effort collapsed after 1846. The decay of national authority and the social order was completed by the Federal War (1859–1864) in which the federalist victory decentralized future civil conflicts among the twenty centralized states. The long task of restoring a central authority over local communities and the dispersed individuals of a largely manorial and pastoral society was initiated in 1870. The full nationalization of social authority in the Venezuelan community was at last accomplished by Juan Vicente Gómez in the quarter century from 1909 to 1935.

Since the death of Gómez in 1935, Venezuela has been moving toward an egalitarian society. Concurrently the nation has been endangered by militarism because its social structure was still in an early phase of reforming into the interest groups of a modern society. Of these the armed forces, at mid-point in their development as a career professional institution, were the best integrated. Subsequent tradition-patterned civilian recourse to violence in this recent period, in the absence of substantial organized civilian groups capable of dominating and stabilizing the political process, reinforced the attraction to the armed forces of the power vacuum left by the passing of caudillism. To this point Dr. Rafael Caldera, leading figure of Venezuela's Social Christian Party COPEI, has stated that "Venezuelans are so accustomed to make the army arbiter of their political contests, that at each moment the most varied groups for the most dissimilar ends attempt to involve the army in new adventures to change our political reality." [14]

2 | SOCIETY IN THE ERA OF
THE CAUDILLO

Venezuelan colonial society was a society of estates, mod-
elled after the Spanish version of the social order still current in most of Europe in the eighteenth century. It was a
society of estates, however, to which a new dimension had
been added by the rivalry of Peninsular and creole and by
the necessity of finding a place for three races and their mix-
tures. The socio-political effects of such a new dimension
probably represent the main influence of the colonial milieu
(frontier) on the society of estates. The historian's hallowed
phrases which narrate the old European conflict of interest
between nobility and king and which recount the growth of
royal power in alliance with the Third Estate must be re-
cast. For the Spains across the seas in the Americas, the historian's concept of the royal person must be enlarged to
admit the officials and residents born in Spain who were also

an influential sector of the American Second Estate along with the creoles and a very modest proportion of mestizos. The royal person thus multiplied into a myriad by segments of the colonial First and Second Estates was able to enter into more direct contact with the multi-myriads of mestizos, pardos, Indians, and slaves as a rival of the patriciate sector of the Second Estate.

Such was the society which was given republican political and social forms upon gaining independence. The imperial government which it succeeded had been in form a highly centralized, bureaucratic, and absolute monarchy— the instinctive goal of the caudillo. The fact that the monarchy's control over Venezuela was limited by difficult communications, a scant dispersed population, and oligarchical personalism in local government also represented the reality of government under a national caudillo. Prior to independence regionalism had developed almost unchecked, despite establishment of a common mainland authority in 1777. Until very recently control of republican government was commonly identified with one or another major geographic segment of the nation. The bosses (*mandones*) of the colonial era represented groupings of interrelated prominent families controlling municipal and provincial governments as well as the lower and appellate courts, so that the role of the higher royal officials was limited. In republican terms the middle and upper classes of colonial society not only possessed an awareness of class and racial separateness, but also were formed into interest groups of recognized personality with fueros.[1]

After mid-eighteenth century the Bourbons in their enlightened despotism enlarged the scope of commerce within the empire and particularly sought to possess the entirety of political authority. In the Venezuelan area the Caracas Company and the new retail monopolies of the government were followed by the first step of unification under the intendancy system in 1776. Consolidation was completed by the creation of the Captaincy General of Venezuela in 1777. Then came the installation of an audiencia on July 19, 1787. These changes were accompanied by a growing tendency among royal officials to make common cause with the Peninsulars and Canarians as well as with the mestizo and mulatto elements of the towns. These latter two elements in colonial society were given access to local office.[2] The increased role offered mixed bloods was probably responsible for a more egalitarian spirit towards each other among whites of different social levels, a phenomenon reported by Alexander von Humboldt.[3] It is a facet of criollismo.

Possibly of greatest importance and most sensitively felt was the royal invasion of the traditional prerogatives and functions of the cabildo and the alcaldes *ordinarios* after 1736. Minor justices (*tenientes de justicia*) were appointed by the crown and given the same competence as alcaldes. A subject could have recourse either to the teniente or to the alcalde in his quest for justice. Moreover, as foci of population were accorded the dignity of villas, they were not authorized the older style of municipal institutions. Instead of cabildo and alcalde, the teniente de justicia and other appointed officials handled civic affairs. Descendants of conquistadors and of first settlers were no longer given preference in municipal appointments,[4] and in the older cities and villas creoles had to share the alcaldías with Peninsulars.

Nineteenth-century Venezuelan society was not a complex structure. Its chief features were a limited population of some 700,000 people in 1825, roughly divisible into an upper class (patriciate or bourgeoisie) of country and town of about 3.5%, middle groups of approximately 7%, a free lower class of roughly 81.5%, slaves about 4%, and uncontrolled Indians of 4%.[5] The largely rural character of the nineteenth-century Venezuelan population has not been questioned. The preceding class distribution was based on an analysis of the 1846 electoral lists. At that time the population was rated at 1,272,155 people, of whom 128,785 (10.1%) were registered as voters. The qualified voters were 75% rural. A third of the voters were literate and 8,798 (6.8%) met the requirements to be an elector. Not quite half the qualified voters cast ballots. It seems likely that a higher percentage of the urban voters exercised their right to vote than did those of the rural areas. An occupation breakdown of the qualified voters gave the following: [6]

Agriculturists	52,686 [rural]
Stockmen	12,457 [rural]
Day laborers	43,169 [⅔ rural]
Mule and donkey owners and drivers	1,155 [rural]
Storekeepers and merchants	5,315 [urban]
Tradesmen	7,801 [urban]
Persons in navigation	2,533 [urban]
Public employees	2,124 [½ rural]
Military, including sergeants and corporals	623 [urban]
Clergy	316 [½ rural]
Physicians and surgeons	110 [urban]
Lawyers	68 [urban]
Procurators	41 [urban]
Teachers	247 [urban]
Students	140 [urban]

The upper and lower segments of rural society were linked together in the traditional patrón-campesino relationship and a common nominal religious identification. They were served by a limited middle sector of public officials and employees which included most military officers and teachers, professional men, parish priests, shopkeepers, artisans, and peddlers. Social mobility existed mainly as the harvest of education, participation in commerce, and political violence. However the ruling groups may have been reconstituted during and after the wars for independence, the colonial social order continued in effect with an upper class interpreting the new political order to serve its own ends.[7] Moreover, if a family's property holdings were on the grand scale of the Monágas or the Tovar families, sufficient economic power, personnel, and equipment for violence existed to protect the family from the full effects of unsuccessful political adventures. Thus the Tovars in 1858 were still rated the largest landowners in Venezuela despite the wars for independence and subsequent civil conflicts.[8] It would appear, therefore, that major exchanges in property ownership occurred more commonly in the middle and lower ranges of estate sizes than in the largest.

The bulk of the population "remained in status quo because it was impossible to accomplish in a day the necessary fusion of the different elements comprising its mass so that wholly and equally it might enter into the enjoyment of political liberty and equality offered it by the constitution."[9] During the 1820's there were few fully qualified citizens, and an English editor in Ecuador who had also served in Caracas commented in 1828 that Gran Colombia's main traits were "a military aristocracy dangerous to lawful authority, dangerously widespread seeds of dissension, institutions without roots in the hearts of the citizens, customs of self-interest frequently opposed to order and even to liberty." [10] Bolívar had also stated, "Unfortunately among us the masses can do nothing. Some vigorous spirits do it all and the multitude follows audacity without questioning the justice or the crime of the leaders, but abandon them then at the moment that others more daring surprise them. Such is the public opinion and the national vigor of our America." [11]

The era of caudillism was associated with an overwhelmingly agricultural as well as ranching and extractive economy, complemented by a foreign-trade-oriented financial and commercial sector. The classes of this strongly manorial and pastoral society were related to such contrasting elements as market and subsistence parts of the economy, the ruling groups and the governed, the educated and the uneducated. Although the correspondence was not wholly exact, the upper and middle sectors of society were identified with the market economy, the ruling groups, and the educated. They possessed social authority in Venezuela. The remainder of the population was generally illiterate, denied a direct political role, and tied to the subsistence economy. The manorial particularism of nineteenth-century Venezuelan society was preserved by the lack of public services and a related absence of community identification. Public services could not be provided by ineffective local governments with inadequate tax revenues, nor could they continue to be supplied in part by the Catholic Church within the very limited role and resources allotted it. Frequent political violence, impunity for crime, and the pervasive awareness of race and class tensions contributed powerfully to social disorder in the nation. It was most visible in the city in peacetime, but in wartime the rural population played the major roles of victim and aggressor.

Venezuelan pressure and interest groups provided no stabilizing framework in society during the caudillesque era. Independence had dissolved the special jurisdictions under fuero which had given them consistency, place, and function in colonial society. Juan Beneyto in sketching the broad framework of the social order in Spanish America for the nineteenth century noted the inheritance of the corporative spirit of Spain which he described as a "deformation of the medieval system of orders and in contradiction with the providential sense of [the middle ages]." [12] What had occurred, of course, was the conversion of one-time medieval classes and corporations into something equivalent to the pressure groups of a more modern society. In Spain and its empire these groups had enjoyed a variety of privileges and jurisdictions which set them apart from the bulk of the population and provided the channels of contact between the more or less powerful elements of the population and the government. The arrangement delayed and diluted the development of effective inter-group opinion, retarded formation of parties or factions, contributed to the stability of imperial government, and enabled the crown to serve its subjects while controlling them on a basis of divide and rule. In Venezuela the structure was not as complex nor as fully developed as in the more populous parts of the empire. Full conquest and effective internal settlement had been the work of the seventeenth and eighteenth centuries from bases occupied in the sixteenth century. Neither the economy of Venezuela nor the scant density of its population required the variety and vigor of similar institutions in other parts of the empire. [13]

The highest echelon of the creoles, the colonial equivalent to the Spanish grandee, was a small patriciate of interrelated families of country and town commonly referred to
as the *mantuanos.* Despite the fact that there were some
families with noble titles among them, the mantuanos
should not be referred to as an aristocracy in the European
sense, a label denied them by Alexander von Humboldt and
by modern Venezuelan scholars.[14] The creoles, led by the
mantuanos, persistently opposed any innovation by government which threatened even indirectly their privileged position and economic activities. They resisted the enlightened
despotism attempted by the Bourbon dynasty which included erosion of the private and public law of the empire,
a whole juridic system, by dispensations based on a regular
schedule of fees. Ots Capdequi has concluded that "few
facets of economic interest to subjects, or of simple social
vanity, . . . susceptible to exploitation by the Treasury,
escaped the canny editors of the schedule." [15] Thus the
mantuanos bitterly assailed economically based racial
equality provided by the real cédula of *gracias al sacar*
issued for Venezuela in 1795.[16]

Fragmented into local oligarchies, the mantuanos dominated cabildos but had failed in sedition and revolution in
defense of their interests.[17] Nevertheless, the Spanish governmental crisis imposed by Napoleon in 1808 caught the
empire short in dominant peninsular authority. Consequently, a "handful of aristocrats and lawyers" overthrew
the government in Venezuela despite the loyalty of the people.[18] Success of the "handful" derived from the consulado
and from factional alignments linked to it which struc-
tured creole-peninsular rivalry and the friction built into
the imperial system of government. Establishment of the

consulado in Caracas in 1793 instituted the means needed to focus the diffuse mantuano community of interest based on family, common economic activity, and role in local government. Membership in the consulado, distributed among hacendados, *comerciantes*, and *mercaderes*,[19] was broadly inclusive of the legally white population, according to Pons.[20] The mantuanos were able to enlarge their influence in society. Among the hacendados every major family was represented, as were the leading merchants. The consulado provided a forum for the advancement of economic production and trade as well as a locale in which to sharpen the conflict of interest between the creole growers and intellectuals and the Peninsular merchants. The consulado did not survive independence.

Development of two factions in the government of the Captaincy General of Venezuela at the time of the founding of the consulado helped structure creole-peninsular rivalry. Esteban Fernández de León, who was both Intendant of the Province of Caracas and President of the Consulado, and his wealthy hacendado brother Antonio were opposed to the Captain General and the Basque element which still sought to control the economic life of Venezuela even after the termination of the Caracas Company. The Intendant was aided by the Audiencia whose Regent was a rival of the Captain General for preëminence in authority. The lineup of high officials plus the conflicting groups in the consulado provided the organizational structure for a high level oligarchy,[21] equivalent to the establishment of a corpus of creole leadership in the captaincy general.

A major element in the functioning of the colonial political process indicated above was the enjoyment of fuero.

Fueros were a body of privileges, rights, jurisdictions, functions, and obligations accorded a town, corporation, association, class, or individual by charter or law granted by the crown. Such a charter or law might accord a very limited or a broad range of privileges and other elements of exceptional status. Fueros may be classified as those of class (First and Second Estate), professional (economic, religious, military, official), honorary, and associational. Within these categories there were more than thirty types of fueros, among which the more important were the ecclesiastical, military, municipal, guild, commercial, mining, lay religious, and those for some government bureaus. The military fuero, for example, varied according to the grade of personnel and type of unit.[22]

Fuero was, therefore, a system of justice, a special jurisdiction or court to which only an authorized group or person could have recourse for justice. The competence of the jurisdiction varied for each fuero. In case of a conflict between fueros, that is a conflict between jurisdictions, the crown decided which fuero took precedence. For many people, however, fuero placed judicial control over them into the hands of people with fuero, such as military officers, clergy, specific categories of administrators and judges. Thus fuero not only served to distinguish between various categories of people within the First and Second Estates, but also made people of these two estates administrators of justice to those of the Third Estate. One must not confuse multiplicity of jurisdictions, i.e., jurisdictional pluralism, with swift justice. It is true that these jurisdictions converged at one or another appellate level, but conflicting procedural rules and variations in substantive law created a legal labyrinth almost impossibly tangled.

Desire for fuero was a common phenomenon in Spain and Spanish America. Much of Venezuela's white population possessed ecclesiastical, military, commercial, class, or administrative fueros. Venezuelans whom the king would honor with some distinction were given more commonly some one of the degrees of military fuero, indicating the nonprofessional and catch-all traits of one or another type of military fuero.[23] The practices affecting fuero were not limited to Venezuela. In neighboring Nuevo Reino de Granada, to which Venezuela had belonged for some decades in the eighteenth century, the employees in the secretariat of the viceroy sought to dignify their status by obtaining fuero, in this case military fuero. Since the viceroy was also captain-general and a professional military man, the viceroy would have direct jurisdiction over their personal legal problems.[24]

The middle and lower sectors of society enjoyed at least a modicum of fuero through their lay religious associations (*cofradías*) and guilds (*gremios*). The decay of these organizations deprived much of the population of group identification and action to advance their social and economic interests. Gremio came to be no more than a term to refer to artisans as an element of society. The surviving cofradías continued an exiguous existence in a hostile milieu. They faithfully reflected the nearly terminal effects of Bourbon regalism, of social strife in the wars for independence, and of republican regalism informed with European secularism on the religious life and organizations of Venezuela. The cofradía and the gremio lost what they had possessed of fuero, and the fueros of the clergy and the armed forces were sharply curtailed by the mid-1830's.[25]

Thus every level of society lost in the aftermath of independence the greater part of the nonpolitical, professional, economic, religious, and social organisms which had developed during the colonial era in association with church and state, and which had represented or served the individual and his social needs. Conceivably the outlook associated with fueros and the groups served by fuero could have developed into republican-style pressure groups. Their elimination gave validity to such republican-phrased statements as that of Daniel Florencio O'Leary: "The government is maintained by the influence and the power of those leaders that have made independence. Institutions alone have no force. The people is an easily managed machine too ignorant to act for itself. Public spirit is non-existent." [26] Termination of fuero responded to such views as those of Juan de Dios Picón, Deputy from Mérida to the Constituent Congress of 1830. Picón opposed military fuero on the grounds that "it attacked liberty because it inspires a certain pride and superiority which makes some believe they are superior to the rest, that everything is due them, and that all ought to yield to their will . . . it attacks equality because the citizen is equal before the law. . . ." [27]

Nearly complete termination of fuero was not effected by the formation of new interest groups. It was the result of an idealistic egalitarian republicanism more effective than the egalitarianism implicit in Bourbon enlightened despotism. Fuero was first abolished for all of Venezuela in the Constitution of 1811.[28] Effective parties were not formed and the essential substructures for parties were missing in society. The individual, the extended family, and traditional identification of one's self and family with a particular class or social level remained. Desire for wealth, for social status, for political power continued, however, in an exacerbated degree. The illiterate campesinos of the rural regions who helped their caudillos to ascend to one of the several stages of political authority profited little. The upper class of country and town with its foci of interests in Caracas and the capital cities of the provinces or states, when it had not provided the new caudillos from its members, usually transmuted them into representatives of the interests and sometimes of the values of the upper class.[29]

Among the better examples of the process of assimilation of caudillos by the upper class are the careers of José Antonio Páez and Cipriano Castro. The point has been made about Páez by virtually every Venezuelan author who has written on the subject. It has not been made so commonly about Castro, who was "transformed by the Caracan gang into a montage of all the vices," despite his strong personality. By the end of the century the process of assimilation was the basis for the "interrelationships that existed between the governing class and the capitalist class. . . ."[30]

Middle class intellectuals, especially lawyers, provided the secretaries and literacy necessary to so many of the caudillos as public leaders. Generally laic in outlook and oriented in the intellectual confraternity of Masonry, the intellectuals firmly established the secular orientation of public education and other government policy.[31] Thus the caudillos, no matter what their professed political coloration, maintained the traditional imperial control of the administrative life of the Catholic Church despite the latter's struggle for independence and the civil rights of a juridical person.[32] The foreign concessionaires as they entered the scene lobbied constantly, supporting one or another national caudillo in the quest for more favorable terms or in protection of established concessions. When this recourse failed, the concessionaire relied on the superior strength of his country of origin to confer on him a preferred economic status through protection of his rights.[33] The role of the concessionaire and the foreign investor was an important one, and once the period of anarchic caudillism was initiated during the Monágas era it complicated the international relations of Venezuela. The granting of concessions began during the Gran Colombia period, but the major successful grants were made after 1870.

The Venezuelan stage, which had been refitted by the war for independence, was overwhelmed by the incessant struggle among the more powerful elements of the population for control of society, leadership of the state, and possession of government office. The drama of Venezuela's development as a national society would reach in full despotic caudillism the realization of national authority over the locality. Such consolidation of authority made the saddle, rather than the presidential chair, "the true foundation of the republic for more than a century."[34]

II

Independence left only the institutions and practices of local government relatively untouched amidst the wreckage of the empire. Thus Bolívar could observe that he was "creating as it were a republic in this Department of Venezuela in which each center of population and each man is a little world."[35] Erection of republican government upon such a base lacking even rudimentary political party organizations gave the surviving or reconstituted municipal oligarchies the entrée to regional and national power. The carry-over from the colonial ruling groups seemed slight to the aging Marquis del Toro, who lamented in 1825 that "of the people of our time there is left nothing but the shells and sorry remnants of what they once were." [36] Many of the ruling elements in the new republic had risen to higher social station through demonstrated leadership in armed conflict under conditions of social disorder. These elements took over the properties and role of members of the local oligarchies of the colonial era who had departed into exile, had died in warfare, were slaughtered in racial violence, or were ruined by loss of property, capital levies, and pillage. The distribution of public lands and of sequestered royalist properties in lieu of back pay in the years immediately after the gaining of independence furthered the process. Gran Colombia's Acting President Francisco de Paula Santander stated that under the law of July 25, 1823, some 4,800,000 acres had been distributed or offered to claimants in settlement of military pay and allowances, and that more land was being sought by congress for such purposes from the national total of some 640,000,000 acres.[37]

A reconstituted patriciate was the guiding influence in a society held together in the main by the weakening pull of tradition and custom, by the remaining cement of class structure, and by the magnetic force of the national caudillo. Even the opposition acknowledged the lack of the customary means for effective government, to say nothing of strong or of despotic government. The Liberal Party's *El Venezolano* in its first issue in 1840 assessed the general situation in these terms: "The government of Venezuela is nearer a patriarchate than something the world calls a government. Without army, without navy, without policy, without militia, without any element of material force, it has nothing visible for its support. . . . In domestic matters, what does it have? It has moral force and nothing more, the adherence and love which the people have for it." [38]

Nevertheless, the *luces del siglo* were having what was then described as a dissolving effect on Venezuela. The social impact of "thirty years of revolution with republicanism has so be-barbarized and sunk in every way the idea of respective ranks among descendants from those who once claimed such a difference that there is no distinction in this . . . city." [39] Eight years later another reporter commented in similar vein that the "principles of democracy have struck deeper roots in Venezuela than in any other part of Spanish America that I have been in . . . and as a consequence the middle and lower classes are rude and offensive in their general bearing and conduct, especially in Caracas where they are almost exclusively composed of coloured people." [40]

Under the republic membership in the patriciate was open to men who achieved economic or political success. The patriciate maintained its influence and played its role in society by coalescing around caudillos and by working in conjunction with them. [41] A constant trait of nineteenth century Venezuelan politics was the "group or camarilla . . . [which] places in government a so-called strongman to have its being around him like insects around a light." [42] The process had begun by 1824 and its success was manifested after 1830 by the alliance of the patriciate with Páez and a series of measures which underwrote the sanctity of property, instituted absolute liberty of contracts, restricted the benefits of political liberalism to the patriciate of country and town, and guaranteed domestic social order through the organized arming of the patriciate in the militia. [43]

Such legislation reflected attitudes clearly expressed by two property owners in 1821. Ramón Espejo in seeking return of property liberated by the armed forces urged not only his need of it to carry on agriculture, but also "the benignity of our present government strives that no citizen be deprived of his property which it views as a sacred thing." Juan José Rivas Pacheco refused to "believe that the government may permit, I do not say it permits, but not even that it may have the slightest knowledge of disorders that openly attack the valuable right of property. That would be nothing. The worst is that the people, that individuals, that the very enemies of the system are certainly convinced that the government continues the program of despotism that was constantly practiced by the former [government], reducing the people to misery and despair. Nothing is more opposed to the principles of nature and to the beneficent intentions of the Republic than a conduct which even the most barbarous lands would have disapproved." [44] Vigorous punitive legislation for protection of property included generous use of the lash, long jail sentences, and the death penalty.[45]

The colonial mandones, unrestrained by the moderating influence of monarchical government, were transformed in the new republican era into *gamonales,* caciques, and caudillos. The terms *gamonal, cacique,* and *caudillo* designate differing but related qualities of socio-political leadership. They have been used interchangeably by some authors, especially in the characterization of dominant personalities at the lower levels of government. *Gamonal* carries with it an overtone of economic and family basis for local leadership. Of the three terms it most closely approximates *mandón* in its colonial usage. In the republican period the gamonal, as the preceding mandón, was an element of the patriciate which would in the long run play a lesser role in the nineteenth century than in the colonial era. Patrician inability to retain control is explained by Caraccioli Parra-Pérez: ". . . government as well as the nascent opposition were composed of men bound together only by interest or personal discontent, without common doctrine nor any program." [46] The episodic unity manifested in congress was not continuous enough to enable the patriciate to achieve an enduring role as a ruling national oligarchy or plutocracy.

Parra-Pérez has treated at length the relations of Páez with the patriciate, which he calls an oligarchy. More recently Ambrosio Oropeza has analyzed events from 1824 to 1872 as the working out of a conscious bargain between caudillism and oligarchy, which reached a compromise on the basis of mutual need. Oropeza has indicated in his highly patterned treatment of the subject that a split in the oligarchy, represented by the formation of the Liberal Party, eroded the compact until Guzmán Blanco completed the defeat of the traditional oligarchy as a social nucleus in its last feeble rebellion of 1872. The analysis has some merit if the design imposed on events is not given too high relief. Oropeza's equation of the Monágas regime with the *poder militar* reflects traditional misuse of the label.[47]

Caciques and caudillos possessed more of the immediate substance of authority. As a label *cacique* indicated the successful role of leadership on a basis of professional or purely personal gifts in cooperation with an oligarchy. The cacique, rural or urban, was and is a political boss whose will was law, to whom codes and regulations were subordinate, and whose control of the services of government was such they were simply instruments for his use.

Like the caudillo his stay in power depended on his prestige which was manifested in his area by complete control of patronage and of the delegates elected to assemblies and congresses. The institution has been a means by which an oligarchy in control of national government guaranteed its permanence under representative republican institutions. In exchange for despotic local control, the cacique guaranteed deputies to state and national legislatures properly compliant with the will of the oligarchy as expressed through the executive branch.[48]

Caciquismo did not become the core of the political process in Venezuela. Its stunted development was probably a reflection of the failure of the patriciate to win and keep control of national government. Instead the caudillos dominated the patriciate and made the use of violence the key to office and the sanction behind their control of government services and institutions. Sufficient caciquismo existed, however, to contribute to the political and social folklore of Venezuela material for exploitation by Venezuelan authors in the latter part of the nineteenth century and during the twentieth. Thus General Francisco Tosta García in his costumbrista novel, *Don Segundino en Paris,* portrayed a cacique-type described as the "perfect type of parish wise man, Machiavelli of the town, [one] of those village Talleyrands, market-place diplomats with which our America is plagued."[49] Moreover, Don Rómulo Gallegos's famed novel *Doña Barbara* portrays a female cacique, a sufficiently rare specimen in any Western society. In most regions of Venezuela the caudillo was the predominant type and tended to be the chief figure of canton, province or state, and nation whom others had to please. The term *caudillo* generally indicated those men who customarily used a military title and those who functioned primarily as guerrilla leaders in times of political action or stress.[50]

Gamonales, caciques, and caudillos were helped to power by the prompt decay of municipal corporations in the 1820's. Independence had seen the creation of many new units of local government, especially under Articles 15 and 16 of the Law of June 23, 1824, on territorial division.[51] Bolívar considered cabildos "useful as councils for governors" in provincial capitals, but otherwise no more than troublemakers. Some cabildos had fomented sedition and had attempted to seize the sovereign authority of the nation. Those formed after 1820 had simply exasperated citizens living in their jurisdictions by new taxes and the obligation to serve as unsalaried public officials. Many new municipalities did not have enough capable personnel (those who possessed literacy and private income) to enable annual replacement of officials as required by law.[52] For example, Juan Lovera of Chacao was appointed corregidor of Caracas in September 1821. He professed to be deeply honored, modestly asserted that others were more capable than he, and claimed to be unable to serve because he was convalescing from a serious illness. His main reason for asking to be excused from the office, however, was the fact that he did not have the private income necessary to serve a full time public office with decorum. He had neither the house, the furniture, nor the money since he was able to maintain only the barest decency for his family on his professional earnings.[53] Some household heads took more evasive tactics to avoid the honor of public office. Such persons registered as residents in districts in which they owned no property. The national government countered the practice by making such registrants liable for office in the districts in which they registered as well as in that in which they owned property.[54]

Venezuelan authorities commented in 1828 that the usefulness of the municipality had passed, and the government of Colombia was authorized to suppress municipalities at the petition of their respective cantons. Under the aegis of his Organic Decree of August 27, 1828, Bolívar suppressed "the degraded municipal councils" and reorganized the provinces.[55] A meeting of 23 delegates, all vecinos and hacendados of the provinces of the Department of Venezuela in 1828 resolved that elective municipal offices ought to be abolished because the municipalities "did not have the qualified men necessary to perform duties that are viewed as an insupportable burden obliging vecinos to desert their places and for these reasons others must be asked, others that have to care for their own affairs in order to provide for the subsistence of themselves and their families." Elected officials ought to be replaced by a judge and administrator appointed by higher authority.[56] Similar views were formally presented by other municipalities for much the same reasons. Turmero alleged that in the colonial era "the cabildos and attorneys general represented the people," a function of other bodies under the republic. Cabildos were therefore concerned only with a *policía baja* which included public health, cleanliness, other public services, and the fostering of agriculture, industry, and commerce. The people of Turmero concluded that the most essential need was an adequate administration of justice rather than a cabildo.[57] Puerto Cabello sought elimination of cabildos that lacked resources and personnel and the replacement with judges equivalent to colonial corregidores and tenientes.[58] To relief of local grievances by abolition of cabildos was joined the pro-secession intent to end the emission of actas contrary to those already sponsored by Páez and his coterie in support of separation from Colombia. The cantons in the absence of cabildos and alcaldes were governed by corregidores appointed by higher authority.[59]

Despite the tinkering with the institutions of government in the 1810–1830 period, independent Venezuela continued to follow the Spanish pattern of government organization with its apparent dispersion or division of functions at the top and its concentration of authority in the hands of an individual or of a municipal corporation in the locality. The principal element in the republican political order was the municipio or parish where the law and administration carried out their dialogue with the citizen. The city and villa continued to function as of old, but their once wide-ranging authority over the countryside was ended. At mid-century the typical rural unit possessed its scantily peopled village with the standard plaza, a church, a court building, and a jail. Local government was administered by a *junta de policía* of two justices of the peace (*jueces de paz*) and a legal agent. Local public office was onerous and generally unsalaried. The two apparent leaders in local life were the parish priest and judge. According to the sardonic description of Fermín Toro the pastor had an entourage of pious people, of beggars and indigents, and of holiday seekers whose chief interest was observing with fiesta the thirty or forty holy days each year. The judge had his clique of bribe-givers, perjurers, falsifiers of documents, and ambulance-chasers. Active political life of a peaceful sort was taken care of by landowners and merchants who voted their tenants and retainers.[60] In 1850 parish judges (*jueces parroquiales*) were added to local government to serve solely as judges. The justice of the peace was the rural equivalent of an alcalde and in the absence of a parish judge also served in a judicial capacity.[61]

In 1880 the role of the pastor had diminished in local society and he was lacking in many parishes. The junta de policía had been replaced by commissioners in city wards and in the *caserios* and *veredas* of the countryside and by the *jefe civil* (civil chief) of the municipio. The jefe civil of cantón had become the jefe civil of the district, and the governor of province had been made subordinate to a president of a state. Cabildos or *consejos* were found in cantonal (district) and provincial seats of government, as well as in state capitals.[62] The *asiento* or *hato*, the residence and livestock handling center of the ranch owner, was a focus of population and of actual social authority outside the formal skeleton of political structure established in the constitution and the laws.

III

The Venezuelan people were ill served by their lawful institutions of government. Páez, despite his role as maximum chief of the Venezuelans, and those working with his government could not come up to the unsatisfactory operational standards the body politic had known in colonial times. The decline is most clearly seen in local government. The annual reports of the provincial governors to their assemblies in the last years (1844–1846) of Páez's influence noted the lack of literate men to fill unsalaried public offices in parish and canton, as well as the virtual illiteracy of many serving in those offices. Many justices of the peace courts were vacant for lack of capable men. Local government and its services were ill housed. Suppression of some cantons was urged because of chronic inability to staff their offices. Equally significant was the social role attributed by one governor to militia duty. He saw in it a means to draw into the villages from time to time the population dispersed in the bush and the grasslands, involving them in some degree in community activity and dependence. He felt it necessary to remind them of their membership in society and to moderate the uncouthness produced by a solitary, appetitive, asocial existence.[63] Humboldt has commented on that long-term condition. He noted that many Peninsulars and creoles lived in the country, enjoying the liberty peculiar to a scanty dispersed population without interest in government because the officials could not get at them.[64] Governor Miguel Marmión of Guayana had reported "many poor families, dispersed people, lost to society, without village or town residence, rootless and with no visible means of support. . . ."[65]

The anarchy of the 1846–1870 period added to other pre-existing conditions tends to support the notion that organized social authority was decaying towards a level ascribed by Sarmiento to the Argentine pampa: "Society had disappeared completely: there remained only the assembled feudal family. There being no society, every kind of government was made impossible. The municipality did not exist, the local services could not be maintained and civil justice had no means of getting at the delinquent."[66] Even the effort to make local office attractive had unfortunate results according to the commentary of the time. When the Province of Aragua authorized a monthly salary of fifty pesos in 1850 for *jefes políticos* (an alternate term for jefe civil) of cantons, a swarm of office seekers was attracted who had no income and no bent for work, but who did want to "have fifty pesos for sure, authority to do little, to harass many, and to vex others now and then. . . ."[67] A similar sentiment had been uttered in 1847 about the alcalde "who has taken the sultanic office to vex people and deny rights." [68]

Under such conditions the observations of Sánchez Viamonte on Argentine caudillism seem applicable: "In the hazardous time of our political organization the caudillo was, more than anything, the only form of government possible within the limits of those circumstances. . . . Without the caudillo, the rural population of the provinces . . . counted for nothing. . . . The caudillo gave it personality by personifying it." [69] In similar vein Rivas Vicuña has stated that Venezuela's closely linked caudillism and regionalism are not properly "vices of the people," but rather "simple events that mark the stages toward human perfection, that tend to healthy groupings differentiated in simple functions for the more ordered and efficacious integration towards the social goal" [70]

More recent Venezuelan assessment [71] influenced by the urgencies of the mid-twentieth century is consonant with the views of Bishop Mariano Talavera y Garcés who expressed his dismay at conditions in his speech at the second inauguration of General José Tadeo Monágas. José Tadeo was returning to the presidency after a four-year interval during which his subordinate brother José Gregorio had been president. The bishop said:

Deeds of sorrowful remembrance have been committed during your four years' absence, the effects of which, you in your retirement, could not feel as it has been our lot to do.

[Every evil has afflicted us:] scarcity of the necessaries of life proceeding from well known causes: agriculture in a deplorable state of prostration arising out of motives of which you are not ignorant: whole families reduced to impoverished circumstances: demands by foreign powers, accompanied by threats: disease and epidemics which have decimated and even destroyed one of every five of the population of several towns and villages: the absolute absence of every police regulation: convulsions of the earth, which in obedience to the immutable laws of the Creator have swept away hundreds of victims: the deathlike silence of the Press, the only organ through which the people may make known their complaints: the finances of the country exhausted to such a degree that the just exigencies of the public servants of the government, are left unsatisfied: an immense public debt that will weigh down future generations: fraudulent stock jobbing and peculation carried on to a scandalous extent: justice debased: every social tie violated: indefinite portions of the community menaced with death: midnight murder and robbery: civil dissensions: opinions which clash with each other: reciprocal odium: political parties that scorn to be reconciled: citizens and military men, who from aberration of political feelings, are now thrown upon a foreign soil where they are eating the bread of charity in exchange for that which they had gained by their blood: and what is still more afflicting, civil war . . . which has produced the deplorable fratricides which cause humanity to groan in anguish.

Behold, Illustrious General, a passing but melancholy sketch of the evils you are called upon to remedy—the profound wounds you are expected to heal.[72]

The British legation's translator of the bishop's address was less discreet:

. . . There is no claim on the government of Venezuela that is ever paid to the original creditor, except such creditor be a foreigner who is supported by the Representative of his country and such Representative in his turn, supported by his Government, thus causing such claim to assume an international character. But the unfortunate natives, whether military men, civil officers, or otherwise, are inevitably put off at the treasury on application being made by them for their pay, salary, or other sums justly due to them, by the stereotyped Venezuelan words, *"no hay,"* and, *"no hay,"* an equivalent for, "there is no money," is the only satisfaction they can ever get. But as the immense majority of these claimants, a majority of at least 90%, are poor men with families to support, who cannot purchase food with "*no hay,*" they are compelled, in order to avoid starvation, to seek for one of the members of the Monagas family (the sons, brothers, uncles, aunts, cousins, sons-in-law, etc. etc., are very numerous; indeed some of them have only lately discovered their affinity after having arrived at the age of forty) or else for one of their numerous agents, and of these there are men of all colours and nations; many natives, some Frenchmen, several Germans and even a John Bull or two. To these speculators on joint account with the Monagas family, both male and female, the claim is sold at 10, 20, 40, or 50 per cent—the percentage being regulated by the amount of the wants or the hunger of the unfortunate original creditor. No sooner is the purchase effected than the purchaser demands immediate payment at the treasury, and payment is, of course, immediately made; for what treasurer in Venezuela would dare to refuse payment to a member of the Monagas family; besides which the treasurer himself as well as other privileged employees deal in the same wares.[73]

Under such conditions of disorder and *agiotismo* the ever-present possibility that widespread discontent would explode the class and racial tension endemic in Venezuelan society was realized in the Federal War. Such a conflict had been feared, and a succession of United States Chargés regarded it as inevitable.[74] According to despatches of foreign representatives in Caracas the Monágas regime was despotic and anti-white.[75] Racial tension had been rising rapidly in the 1850's. The colored population of Caracas, for example, was supremely confident towards the whites. French Chargé Levraud cited the arrest of a colored thief in the legation residence. The culprit demanded to be taken before the judge immediately, correctly confident in his prompt release. Levraud attributed to such impunity the "origin of the crimes that desolate the country." [76] The rural sector was no better off. No level or aspect of society was free of social decay, and in the countryside the peons denied all authority, the manumitted led slave rebellions, herds were depleted, and large scale rustling operations were directed from Caracas. The Federal War was the climax of a decade of increasing disorder in society, but the end of the war did not promptly terminate the disorder, which would continue into 1870 before being reduced to manageable proportions. In the late 1860's the disorder provided the excuse for the Blue Revolution of 1868–1869, which was no improvement. Neither Federalist President Falcón nor the Monágas of the Blues dominated the turbulences.[77]

A social revolution had occurred in Venezuela, but its political aims were thwarted. Nor was it proletarian in the modern sense, despite the reported presence of "a number of Frenchmen in this Republic . . . obliged to quit their native country from their extreme Republicanism or Socialist opinions . . . and who encourage . . . any political disturbances by which they may possibly be benefited." [78] Heavy property losses and the death of three per cent of the population in the Federal War followed by several years of rapine and murder effected considerable change in personnel among the ruling elites. The elite outlook was not modified, however, nor was caudillism eliminated. The most important effect was the fusion of the population to the degree that racial conflict would no longer be a major concern in subsequent political violence.

Arcaya has emphasized the replacement of the old leadership by caudillos, most of them of proletarian origin, whose ascent severed their ties with the elements whence they rose. Their bonds of obligation were, instead, with "the group of individuals, their friends and supporters, who constituted their 'prestige.'" [79] These caudillos continued, after Guzmán Blanco's accession to power in 1870, the piratical practices of guerrilla life as a system for "seizing the cattle and horses of peaceful farmers, and for depriving respectable citizens of their property, besides the mal-administration of the laws by incompetent individuals [which] leaves no hope of justice or safety for foreigners in Venezuela." [80]

The preceding British commentary was reinforced by United States reporting in the aftermath of the Federal War. The element of racial conflict did not appear in despatches. The Blue Revolution of 1868, mounted under the leadership of Monágas and Páez, was reportedly the work of the propertied element possessing eighty-five per cent of the wealth. The source did not indicate any variation in composition of the patriciate, nor any significant redistribution of property. To counter the revolution the nearly bankrupt Federalist government allegedly had only the support of the officeholders, profiteers from government contracts, and possibly the army. The government existed on a day by day basis from the daily receipts of the custom house at La Guaira. The banks were closed, and half the improved land of Venezuela lay fallow for want of the labor force impressed into the fighting forces of government and rebel.[81] The overthrow of the Federalist government of General Juan Falcón was followed by the election of 1868, described as free, in which José Tadeo Monágas was elected president for the third time. The generally optimistic report noted as the only problem the danger that the two dozen or so relatives of Monágas would deny the other revolutionary leaders their due rewards by occupying all the best government posts.[82] José Tadeo died shortly after, and his heirs could not retain control.

The internal power structure was clarified very rapidly after the defeat of the Salazar rebellion in 1872, and the incidence of violence was sharply reduced until about 1877 when another period of regression in political and social order began to develop. The departure of Guzmán Blanco from office in 1877 was followed by a "spirit of insubordination to local authorities, but in no way combined with any manifestation of hostility towards the President [Linares Alcántara] of this Republic . . . only having resulted in an appeal to arms in three of [the states], however, and appears to have arisen entirely from a determination no longer to submit to the putting in practice of the restrictive and coercive doctrines, inculcated by General Guzmán Blanco; tranquillity has been restored in most of the disturbed states referred to by the dissemination, by means of Delegates despatched direct from the central government, of ideas in harmony with the popular aspirations of the moment, . . . and [Linares Alcántara's] determination to adjust his policy to the democratic yearnings of the people." [83] The unexpected death of Linares Alcántara in 1878 anarchized the country. A variety of hopeful successors organized their followers for the race to the presidency, but General Gregorio Cedeño "had the better situation" and prepared the way for Guzmán Blanco's return to power in 1879.[84] Guzmán Blanco was never again as securely seated as in the 1870–1877 period, however. He needed, increasingly, the support of Joaquín Crespo who emerged as the most successful caudillo during the decade after the passing of Guzmán Blanco.

By the end of the century things appeared to be reverting to the anarchy of 1846–1870 as the leading caudillos fought for predominance. "We have, yes, the civil wars, looting, disorders, and useless shedding of blood [that] are the consequence of the ineptitude of the chiefs; during peace the Administration acts without plan and in ignorance, because no attention was paid to the knowledge and experience of individuals but to their merits as partisans of the respective political cause whose desires must be satisfied." [85] According to the United States Minister the masses continued to count for little, while people of property, politicians, and leaders of the army constituted the ruling groups.[86] President Andrade from his exile in Puerto Rico in 1900 declared that Venezuela had many politicians who would do anything to live off the public treasury as was their custom.[87] The business community, hostile to President Castro's forced loans, hoped Venezuela's creditors would take over collection of customs because it would end the booty—the main cause of revolutions—and bring peace.[88] Peace was the chief desideratum since prolonged anarchy had brought the economy to a standstill. By 1902 the hungry were flocking into Caracas to join the hungry there because their fields were stripped clean by the troops of both sides. Only half the families of Caracas were reported to have one good meal a day.[89]

From time to time the hard-pressed governments of Venezuela had attempted to check the incidence of violence by limiting the possession of arms. The wars for independence had left weapons widely dispersed in the population. Páez had continued the dispersion of government arms with the formation of the militia and granting of permission to reliable militiamen to keep their arms at home.[90] Moreover, the intent of the militia laws of the 1830–1846 period was to make the militiamen provide their own arms. The president asserted to congress in 1836 that one cause for delay in defeating the recent rebellion was poor distribution of war matériel. He asked for a completed militia organization whose members would keep their arms at home.[91] Each subsequent conflict saw the dispersion of a good part of the national arsenal into private hands. In 1872 Guzmán Blanco ordered immediate return of all government weapons "furnished to the different Generals . . . and troops have been despatched to the different districts to enforce compliance with it, if necessary." [92] He also prohibited trade in powder, rifles, muskets, and other munitions. In 1873 the government reserved to itself the importation of all arms. The same measures were repeated in 1885 and 1886, and the wearing of arms in towns and the Federal District was prohibited in 1889. After 1890 the administrations tried to improve training of the armed forces and limited the right to bear arms as a means of controlling violence. The collection of government arms again widely dispersed in private hands was ordered in 1893 and repeated in 1896. It was again necessary at the end of 1898.[93]

At the end of the nineteenth century little apparent change had occurred in the structure of society, yet certain social, economic, and political trends were already observable. They forecast the state of Venezuelan society at the present moment. Racial conflict as a major stress in society had terminated. Anarchic caudillism was ending as the tyranny adequate to that purpose was being imposed. The role of the economically active had been largely limited to economic things. All of this had come about as the result of Venezuelan activity, not of foreign imposition or intervention. The increasing involvement of Venezuela in international economic activity would simply hasten the process of laying the foundation for the reconstruction of the pressure groups essential for the active effective representation of all elements of the population in the functioning and leadership of society.

3 | ON CAUDILLISM

In his introduction to a volume of quotations from Venezuelan authors on the subject of caudillism, Virgilio Tosta
has summarized the views of selected writers in other Latin
American nations on the causes of caudillism. These writers
have attributed the rise of caudillism to geography, racial
mixture, miserable cultural conditions, inherited customs,
or to economic conditions. One writer or another has classified caudillism as a sub-product of independence tempo-
rarily interrupting the colonial civilian tradition of government. The term civilian tradition implies the rule of law.
Much earlier and with a narrower focus than the commen-
taries of Sánchez Viamonte and of Rivas Vicuña quoted in
the preceding chapter, Venezuela's Cecilio Acosta classified
Bolívar as the caudillo *benefactor* who supplied the missing
political institutions.[1] Some decades later Vallenilla Lanz

pointed out the apparent unwillingness of a newly independent people to trust society to the rule of law and its
preference for the ministrations of a strong personality.
Accordingly, he perceived in caudillism and the caudillo
for Venezuela "the only force for social conservation, re-
peating the phenomenon that men of science have observed
in the first stages of integration of societies: the chiefs are
not elected but impose themselves." [2] Mario Briceño Iragorry subsequently stated that nineteenth-century caudillism "represented the natural state of a society in which
cantonal gamonalism aroused by the militarization of the
revolutionary war, took anarchic form." [3]

Caudillism may be defined as the union of personalism
and violence for the conquest of power. It is a means for the
selection and establishment of political leadership in the
absence of a social structure and political groupings adequate to the functioning of representative government. The
practice and technique of caudillism, developed during the
wars for independence, were based on those of the colonial
oligarchies as modified by the regressive effects of irregular
civil conflict. Colonial personalism had operated within the
imperial rule of law. During the wars for independence it
was given over to violence by the formation of guerrilla
units with recognized spheres of influence. Guerrilla leaders
exercised local and regional political leadership as a natural
right and allied themselves with royalist or patriot forces
as conviction or circumstances might dictate.[4] As caudillos
they expressed in their persons the capabilities and aspirations of their followers on whom they relied. Such leaders
had scant concern for development of joint action with
similar forces in adjacent areas.[5] Their outlook in government was consonant with that of patriot military officers

appointed to local political offices to compel the citizen to supply conscripts, matériel, and money for the war effort. The doctrine of the situation was formulated in 1818 by Francisco de Paula Santander, Granadian commander in the Province of Casanare under Bolívar:

The *jueces mayores* [higher judges] in their cantons are sub-delegates of the government or justice, as the commandants are of military authority. Between the one and the other the best harmony ought to exist, without discourtesy in their dealings. The jueces mayores have sole knowledge in civil and political affairs and the commandants in those of war; but when these have an order from competent authority to do something in the military sphere, like an ingathering of men, cattle, foodstuffs, and other such, the jueces mayores must obey them without any excuse so that they never delay the actions directed towards the security of the republic. This [instruction] will serve as a general rule.[6]

In practice, however, with the bulk of the male population under arms or dispersed on farm and ranch the local civil officials were effectively subordinate to the local commandant.

Royalist officers were assigned similar duties in the areas they dominated. Pleading the necessities of warfare, the Spanish military command's higher echelon ignored the policies and decisions of restored civil authority. That practice was evident in 1812 in Venezuela under Monteverde, and even after being rewarded with the rank of Governor, Captain General, and President, Monteverde would continue to ignore the audiencia.[7] General Morillo was no improvement in this matter either in Venezuela or in Nueva Granada. Most developments during the struggle for independence contributed in some way to the depreciation of civil authority and to the denial of the usual ends served by the rule of law.

Guerrilla leaders, whether formally commissioned or not, retained their predominance in their chosen areas. As Rivas Vicuña observed, "the caudillos who divide up the booty win out over the great builders of victory." [8] Thus Bolívar, who made an army out of a collection of guerrilla groups, was sacrificed by these one-time guerrilla leaders and their associated regional interests in their determination to exercise political authority. The guerrilla force or armed faction would remain the means of action of these men and their successors. Such forces were called into being as occasion demanded by the caudillos whose effectiveness as political leaders was directly related to the size of the factions they could generate by a simple act of will. The force thus created was an instrument, not an end in itself nor an institution. It would vanish after defeat, or after victory become the new roster of public officials with salaries and perquisites.[9]

Caudillos came from all levels of society and regularly made the interests of the upper class their own. The latter element became evident with the reorganization of government in the wake of independence through the laws passed by the Congress of Angostura (1819–1820), the Congresses of Colombia (1821, 1823–1827), and the decree handed down by José Antonio Páez on January 13, 1830, founding an independent Venezuela by separating it from the first Republic of Colombia. The latter document provided for indirect elections and limited suffrage by requiring literacy and property qualifications. The situation was basically unchanged by the election law of 1847 which established universal suffrage, but maintained the indirect electoral process and raised the qualifications for the role of elector.[10] It seems clear that the instability of property and evidence of social change brought into being in Venezuela by class and racial conflict associated with the war for independence had been checked by 1830. In Venezuela the cooperation of caudillos and the upper class had been facilitated by the common opposition to authority located in Bogotá in the 1820s, but that cooperation did not end with the secession of Venezuela from Gran Colombia.

Caudillism as a system of political leadership for the state was an inherently unstable hierarchical arrangement, a structure composed of a network of personal alliances cemented together by community of interest, by force of personality, by ties of friendship and even of family. The scaffolding was enveloped in the brittle stuff of popular acceptance. What stability it possessed was due to the role of political office and especially of the officer corps of the militia in systematizing relationships among the caudillos. As a political system it imposed limitations on the authority of the caudillo effective in inverse ratio to the degree of dominance achieved by the caudillo over his associates.

Caudillos were the natural leaders of a society whose colonial order was destroyed before the bases for an independent society had taken firm shape. Up to mid-nineteenth century the higher ranking combat-trained beneméritos, many of whom became members of or reverted to the landowning upper class after 1825, were the instruments and leaders of rival political groups as a right earned by their part in the making of a nation. They were augmented and, as their numbers were thinned by death or failure, they were replaced by non-veteran caudillos, men who generated their own support, and would in time fight to the top. They would in their turn undertake the difficult task of remaining there by seeking a solid political base in *continuismo* or in puppetry and financial support in the budget and in the patriciate.[11] José Antonio Páez by his *virtu* and his brilliant career as guerrilla leader, as subordinate to Bolívar, and as Superior Military and Civil Chief of Venezuela, had established by 1827 his personal authority over much of what would be the nation of Venezuela. He became the archetype of the caudillo, perhaps in his own despite. He was never able to eliminate caudillism in Venezuelan society.[12] It has been aptly pointed out that after Páez subdued the rebels of the War of the Reforms in 1835 the presidents regularly came forth from conflict and were with one or another exception the personification of the guerrillas.[13]

Caudillos manifested their capacity for leadership by violence, the successful practice of which proved the quality of their *virtu* by dominating and holding the wills of other men. Violence involved a direct assault on authority by volunteer armed forces. A prerequisite to the violent transfer of power was the decay of the incumbent's personal influence and prestige which enabled an ambitious individual and a handful of supporters to initiate the overthrow of a national or a regional caudillo. The process has been described as "the classic regional [political] avalanche brought into being by defections of lesser caudillos," whom Antonio Guzmán Blanco contemptuously characterized as "*macheteros* representing force, ignorance, and aguardiente." [14] The element of prestige attracted the attention of the British Minister in 1848, who noted that the defeat of Páez at Cambero by a llanero force deprived him "of that prestige which has hitherto been the main source of his political power in Venezuela; namely, the belief that the 'llaneros' or inhabitants of the plains of Apure could alone be kept under restraint by his influence while they were ever ready at his beck to overturn any government whose existence might be disagreeable to him. . . ." [15] Later in the century a foreign reporter passed on a Venezuelan comment: "When [the politicians] lose power or capacity, the change is sudden. I can show you three ex-Generals in rags in the plaza." [16]

The effectiveness of the lesser caudillos of locality and state lay in their ability to generate at need armed support from the population. Those associated with the national government enjoyed a legal right to call on the militia units in times of crisis.[17] A caudillo in opposition depended on his peons, tenants, relatives, friends, or other supporters to provide the initial attacking force.

Caudillos were "gunmen or paladins," formed by their milieu. "The people admired their energy, pride, and informality. They shared with the chiefs the cassava and veal of the revolutions. The people were secure within the sheltering shadows of their big compadres; they knew their folk justice with its anti-oligarchic and egalitarian character." Caudillos were "chiefs of a following [*mesnada*] and under the wide-boughed trees sat the provincial generals determining the interests of a whole tribe, [generals] who put on urbanity when they came to Caracan congresses or drank their brandy in the corridors of the Hotel Saint Armand with their political clientele. . . . Like the condottieri of the Italian cities of the Middle Ages, each one possessed his gang, men that 'can call a halt,' the compadres that keep their arms on the verandas of the ranches." They were chiefs, heads of clans, great landowners, like Diego Colina who could at a word call out the cane cutters of the southern sierra in the Coro area, or like General

illo who could draft a thousand men from his
~ties,[18] or like the Tellerías who through family
~ most of the higher and many of the middle
~ts of state government could use the resources of the State of Falcón.[19]

Venezuelan caudillism developed an imprecise pattern.
Anyone could volunteer for the role of caudillo. It required
ambition, the simple will to command, a sense of grievance,
or the conviction that change had to be made in government. Caudillos depended on the three leading elements
of society. Rural landowners provided supplies and much
of the manpower, albeit not always willingly. Professional
men manipulated the ideology, formed programs, and made
plans. The commercial and financial sector of the towns and
cities generated funds and the hardware of war.[20] A caudillo
of the various levels of government (national, regional, state
or provincial, district or cantonal, and municipality or
parish) could come from any one of the three elements or
from the campesinos or laboring segment of the population.
As leaders with command over political action units, a
caudillo and his subordinates normally took military titles
commensurate with their evaluation of their services. The
caudillo was primarily a politician, however, and provided
the vigor and character of governmental action in the area
he dominated.

In his training lectures on Moral Education in 1937, Lt.
Col. Manuel Morán sharply contrasted the nature and traits
of the military institution with those of the multitude led
by a caudillo:

The multitude is characterized by psychological incoherence.
. . . Each person [in it] loses his personality under the influence
of the caudillo. . . . The multitude is suddenly assembled under the pressure of an event. . . . [It] has no tradition, it be-

longs to the passing hour, it ends without patrimony. . . . The caudillo of a collectivity is an individual who has a vigorous personality and an enormous prestige, natural or acquired; his main means of action [on the collectivity] are affirmation and repetition. . . . In order for the multitude to accept the ideas presented it, they must be presented in bloc in simple form without need to explain their derivation. Thus [the multitude] listens preferently to those that have fixed ideas and always repeat the same things. . . . The role of the caudillo of a multitude is generally ephemeral. . . . [In defeat] the multitude is a prisoner of fear and panic and the caudillo finds himself abandoned. . . . To abandon a caudillo in misfortune is the general rule of public life. . . . The success of a caudillo is measured by the degree of fanaticism he inspires in the mass he attracts. . . . Fanaticism that collapses entails the end and the dispersal of the multitude, the abandonment of its caudillo.[21]

Illiterate and nearly illiterate caudillos were numerous and they depended on their secretaries to provide the literacy needed for their official functions. The secretary may have been the actual proponent of the uprising which brought the caudillo to power or to the end of his career. Thus Mariano Picón-Salas has pointed out that Don Felipe Larrazábal, musician and author, wanted to dominate a caudillo. He persuaded the literate Matías Salazar to rebel against Guzmán Blanco in the hope that Salazar would make him his all-powerful minister.[22] Similarly Vallenilla Lanz has stated that the Farfán brothers, guerrilla leaders of the wars for independence and unquiet rural bosses thereafter, rebelled again in 1838, using any pretext furnished them by their secretary.[23]

Secretaries were generally intellectuals, of whom Mario Briceño Iragorry has written that they have done more harm to Venezuela than the generals: "The old warrior was usually a fresh and simple man who understood the use of arms as a natural means of expressing his personality and as the sure way to gain control of the means of wealth. Such a warrior—valiant, generous, cheerful—who might be Jacinto Lara, Juan Bautista Araujo, Gregorio Riera, Aquilino Juárez, José Ignacio Pulido, had at his side when he took power a court of docile intellectuals who adjusted the laws to the will of the strongmen or who advised him to rebel to alter the public order." Such a role was known as Urbanejismo after Diego Bautista Urbanejo who told President Monágas that the constitution may serve any purpose.[24]

The need served by the intellectuals was strongly emphasized by Luis Level de Goda who was inextricably immersed in caudillism. After the triumph of the Federal Revolution "almost all the governments of the localities were headed by generals, some so common and ignorant and even barbarous that they did not know how to read and write, but they were cherished by the federal caudillo." [25] Even the archetype of Venezuelan caudillism who once approved Morillo's decimation of lawyers came to value that significant sector of the intellectuals, as "indispensable to formulate adequately for the benefit of caudillos and government officials not only liberty but also tyranny." [26]

Venezuelan caudillism functioned through and around formal constitutional government. The government was representative, republican, with balanced and separate branches. The rule of law was provided for. All this was respected as long as it was convenient to the needs of the caudillos.[27] There was nevertheless a constant expectation that regularly organized political movements channeling public opinion and participation in the political process might come into being. There were the usual two broad currents of political opinion, Liberalism and Conservatism, which provided the necessary comfort of rationalization of action. The Liberal Party was organized in 1840 by some of the Caracan intellectuals known as liberals in the 1820s and who had waged an unremitting campaign against Colombia. Among the organizers was the political chameleon Antonio Leocadio Guzmán. The Conservatives were simply those elements of the population who had aligned themselves around Páez during the disintegration of Colombia and the formation of Venezuela. But parties as organizations did not prosper. "They almost always appeared in the form of personalist clienteles, cacique-led, free of ideological conviction, which the military factions encamped in power replaced with their guiding force." [28] The modern commentator has missed the point that these same *clienteles personalistas, caciqueles, exentas de savia ideológica* transformed themselves into armed elements at need, that they were the *facciones militares* of his analysis.

It was most natural, then, that political accident, family ties, economic interests, and the patrón-campesino relationship commonly determined the position or views of most people about Liberalism and Conservatism. A few intellectuals, the clergy, and the devout were intensely earnest in ideological matters, but there was in fact no precise ideological division between the two movements. Highly varied groups operated within the two political currents at local, state, regional, and national levels of political organization. Caudillos paid due reverence to republican procedures by frequent revision of the constitutions which did not reflect any basic structural change in the political process until the Constitution of 1946. The charters were little more than legislative enactments of political ideals and

of procedures of government deemed useful to facilitate
and dignify the exercise of power. Only since 1936 has the
gap between political process and the forms and procedures
of government established in the constitution begun to
narrow significantly.

Of the modern forms of government, the presidential type
of republican government most satisfactorily contributes
dignity and constitutionality to the caudillo. The presidency of Venezuela became for the most part but a
euphemism for extra-legal personal authority vested in a
more or less charismatic leader. These caudillos were politicians and bosses who imposed their will as the orienting
force in the several levels of government. They held leadership until forcibly removed and new victorious caudillos
were given the accolade of public acclaim, the consent of
the governed. Fermín Toro (1807–1865), who witnessed the
evils of Monágan despotism and nepotism (1847–1858), said
in an 1858 speech that Venezuela's "institutions have been
commonly dictated by power, not by the national will. Public opinion has been no more than the echo of a man and the
flag of the people a name." [29] In the same vein Tomás
Lander, one of the organizers of the Liberal Party, wrote in
catechetical form: "And what is the nation in the eyes of
its powerful ones? A mummy, an inert and embalmed
body . . . , a tool . . . , a toy. . . ." [30]

The cynicism of the electoral system is revealed by British and Venezuelan sources. In 1877 Guzmán Blanco, while
completing his first period of presidential service, would
not let chance determine his successor:

The candidature for the presidency of the Republic lies between the Generals Zavarse and Alcántara, presidents respec-

tively of the States of Falcón and Guzmán Blanco, eight or nine other Generals in favour of whom a few votes were inscribed by order of General Guzmán Blanco, for the purpose of demonstrating the extent of the freedom of opinion in which, however, not a man in the country believes; and the Generals in question being now called upon by the Press to comply with a constitutional duty and show a due respect for the aspirations of the majority! ! ! by transferring the votes bestowed upon them to one or the other of the two Generals above referred to! ! !

Meanwhile General Guzmán Blanco besides having had himself elected Rector of the University of Caracas, so as to enable him to exercise personal supervision over the professors and students and most intellectual classes of the capital, has also had himself elected president of many of the states of the union; having taken the oaths as President of those of Guarico, Barquisimeto, and Yaracuy, before the High Federal Court, declaring at the same time however his resolution of never exercising the supreme authority in any one of them; six hundred troops having been marched up from the State of Guarico, of which General Crespo, now Minister of War, has been until now President, to garrison this capital, it being worthy of remark, also, that most of the men belonging to the disbanded bodyguard of General Guzmán Blanco have had land allotted to them upon or around an estate of his a few miles from hence; with a view it would seem of retaining them within call.[31]

President Joaquín Crespo was even more outspoken in a letter to Guzmán Blanco, November 7, 1885, as the latter was preparing to return to the presidency: "By one of those providential intuitions of our glorious Liberal Party, public opinion in the States of the Federation has been forming sympathetic situations that have coincided perfectly with our manner of thinking, entrusting the direction of affairs to men truly competent and reliable friends of yours and mine."[32] Vicente Lecuna has neatly summed up the situation: "Active life and independent initiatives [in the nation]

were only manifested in war. When the regime was established the nation turned itself into a neutral mass." [33]

The caudillo depended almost wholly on his personal influence, his prestige, until the time of Guzmán Blanco. By
that time the example of the Liberal Party and the desire
for longer tenure in office at the several levels of government made the organization of a more permanent personal
faction a task of immediate concern for the successful caudillo. The militia upon which both Páez and Monágas had
relied from 1830 to 1858 had during the same period become anyone's political instrument. A new more certain
means for stability in political leadership was desired and
sought in political organization after the conquest of office.
The factions formed by the caudillos were generally known
by the names of their organizers, but they were identified
as Liberal or Conservative, terms which designated a community of outlook which at times possessed no more substance than a current of opinion and at other times the
greater solidity of a movement. In accord with these indications, Guzmán Blanco tried to build a personal following
in the 1873–1877 period.[34] In the same decade, General
Eugenio Leopoldo Machado reorganized the Liberal Party
in the region of Táchira and remained its chief figure for
some years, and when General Morales took over the State
of the Andes in 1897 he hastened to build his party.[35] "As
was standard, in Falcón, General Riera set himself at the
head of the historic party which had had for leader his illustrious father General José Gregorio Riera. . . ." [36] Cipriano
Castro did not neglect his political homework in Los
Andes.[37] Such parties were personal political structures
whose fate was linked to that of the caudillo.

As his third period of direct leadership (1886–1888) drew

to an end, Guzmán Blanco hoped that the Liberal Party would become a true political organization. His hopes were thwarted, however, since the existing party structure was not designed for that purpose.[38] The party was still a network of alliances and personal loyalties among caudillos whose hierarchy reflected a "pecking order" determined by such factors as personality, economic strength, and successful violence. In the end the system of caudillism was transformed into a centralized personal despotism by Juan Vicente Gómez, the most complete caudillo in Venezuelan history. He eliminated regional, state, and local caudillos by abolishing the militia, and by building a professionally trained national army led by career officers. He replaced the caudillesque alliances of his predecessors with the more tightly knit personalism of caciquism linked to a rapidly developing bureaucracy. While gaining great personal wealth, Gómez acquired for the government an income independent of the propertied and professional groups. His caciques, his bureaucracy, his army, and an uncontrolled source of government income provided the means to subdue the caudillos, install a Draconian peace. Gómez re-created in Venezuela something similar to the oligarchic personalism of colonial times, dominated by an irresponsible absolutism of authority unknown to the monarchy.

II

Venezuela's caudillos dominated the political scene until a new economic base and redefinition of interest groups began to contribute the substance proper to representative government and the rule of law. Restoration of professional military standards which began towards the turn of the

century and initiation of professional schooling heralded
the passing of the caudillos and their uprisings in the provinces. It would usher in the capture of government by professionally trained garrisons. This transition was facilitated
by foreign investment which valued order and stability.[39]
The coup d'état scarcely disturbs the daily round of affairs.
Nevertheless, the second stage of development flowing out
of the entry of large-scale foreign capital investment was
the generation of economic growth and the rise of modern
broad-gauge pressure groups which normally provided the
means to limit and then to eliminate the coup d'état and
militarism.

The national caudillo provided the driving force in national government and in the hierarchy of officials through
which the will of government made its impact on the citizen. The lesser caudillos were secondary motivating forces
in the process of government, bringing their strength to
bear by participation in government or by application of
external pressure on local officials. Moreover, members of
the national congress were caudillos and caciques of the
lower levels of government, or their agents. Relations between congress and national caudillo bore some resem-
blance to that of Audiencia and Viceroy, and congressional
legislation which expressed that relationship became the
republican form of the *auto acordado en real acuerdo*.[40]

The despotic era of caudillism which opened in 1870 did
not achieve full form until 1920. Nevertheless, the accession of Guzmán Blanco to the presidency in 1870 marked
a new orientation in the attitude of national caudillos towards established political customs, labels, and slogans for
their role. Previously the national caudillo had believed in
the symbolic and sacramental effect of the combination of

high military and political titles. The right to social leadership had long been linked to the joint political and military role of governor and captain general in the colonial period, of general-in-chief and president in the war for independence, and of superior (regional) military and civil chief in Colombia.

Investigators who have leafed through the bundles of documents in the Archivo General de Indias for the century preceding 1825 and who have read the *relaciones de mérito* and correspondence on appointments have observed the specialization of function in the lower grades of the Spanish bureaucracy. They have also noted that as the officials advanced out of the middle grades of the bureaucracy in their respective career specialties the officials tended to lose their branch identity and to pass into a pool of administrators from which the crown drew as needed or as the individual successfully petitioned. Naturally the assigned duties did not conflict too obviously with career specialties, and the military officers particularly found higher political office a means of career advancement.[41] Vice President Francisco de Paula Santander, Acting President of Colombia, evidently had that practice in mind when he referred to the military regimen of an absolute monarchy in asking congress in 1823 to organize the armed forces and militia in accord with the political system of a free state.[42] Ots Capdequi has commented on the "much greater infiltration by the military bureaucracy in political offices and even in the merely administrative" in the last years of the empire.[43] It did not mean, however, any change in the codes of law, nor any basic procedural changes. As military men were untrained in civil law they were probably not as sensitive to the erosion of the juridic system implicit in many of the practices developed during the reign of Charles IV. Colonial practice, therefore, formed a natural basis for the Venezuelan military officers to assert their right to public office and leadership in the 1820's. Although Páez ended the practice for the most part in the 1830's, tradition contributed strongly to the adoption of military titles by would-be political leaders who organized their followers to seize and occupy the posts of government.

Involvement of the opinion-making part of the population in caudillesque alliances, the use of political labels, and victory over the displaced government enabled the Venezuelans to accept caudillesque seizure of office and the appropriation of traditional titles of leadership of Venezuelan society. Such acceptance constituted due investiture with the right to express the general consensus and vital force in Venezuelan society. Such consensus constituted an important part of the prestige of any caudillo. The degree of its loss was reflected in the ease or difficulty encountered in the forcible removal of a caudillo from his office or role.

Instability of tenure and abuse of the military title had become commonplace enough by 1870 so that the national caudillos thereafter accorded military titles less and less validity. The political slogans of yesteryear were replaced with variously defined causes. The national caudillo sought group acceptance and individual veneration in new exalted titles such as *El Ilustre Americano,* which congress awarded Guzmán Blanco in 1873 and which replaced his name in official documents. The use of the terms of public gratitude and honor authorized as titles by congress was not new; the abuse was.

The national caudillo was seeking to become an autocrat or enlightened despot based on a modernized society and centralization of authority. Guzmán Blanco made the effort within the established framework of political ideology and practice. His failure led his successors to seek other arrangements for the domination of society. Guzmán Blanco's hunger for adulation has been commented on by his biographers. George Wise has cited examples of despotic conduct and an expectation of unquestioning obedience.[44] Adulation was equally a factor among later national caudillos as shown by reports of cabinet ministers to congress, by the press, and by other publications of the period 1890 to 1935. This aspect of despotic caudillism has been bitterly indicted by Pedro María Morantes.[45] Not even the clergy could escape. Guzmán Blanco in his travels dedicating completed public works was accompanied by the Archbishop who was expected to emphasize the providential role of the president as an instrument of God for the aggrandizement of Venezuela.[46] Mariano Picón-Salas has observed that during the career of Juan Vicente Gómez the preferred form of adulation was the sonnet or the sociological study justifying democratic caesarism.[47] Adulation took not only conceptual forms expressed in addresses, sonnets, and pessimistic sociological studies, but also the material form of financial benefit. The melody of a well-turned phrase when accompanied by the tintinnabulations of *pesos de oro* achieved full symphonic orchestration. President Linares Alcántara, El Gran Demócrata, happily received from congress an award of 100,000 pesos for his thirty years of service to democracy to enable him to found an estate for his heirs.[48]

The changed outlook of the national caudillo was accompanied by inflation in military commissions. The essential worthlessness of military titles as political instruments, perceived first by the national caudillos, enabled them to take advantage of the continuing force of tradition over local political leaders and among the people by awarding military commissions in recognition of political worth. There was little else to award. The older laurels of praise for republican achievement had been debased. Venezuela possessed neither peerage nor Legion of Honor. True political party organizations were wanting and patronage was not linked to adequate legitimate stipends. During the anarchy from 1890 to 1903 there was a ninefold increase in the number of caudillos and caciques with officially recognized military commissions, which increased from roughly 1300 to over 12,000 of all grades. According to United States Minister Loomis these commissioned men were a large group that "lives on politics and its mutations and to them a revolution means meat and drink." [49]

Inflation in the numbers of military grades has usually been associated with the end of wars as governments reward services of officers in the armed forces, but the practice was neither continuous nor unlimited. Bolívar was probably overgenerous in the years 1826–1830, but the Venezuelan congress in 1830 adopted an ascetic policy for military promotion. Consequently the epoch of inflation of military grades really began with the ascent of José Tadeo Monágas to power in 1847. Disillusionment with high military rank among the national caudillos was probably produced by the fact that between 1859 and 1864 some 108 men were commissioned generals-in-chief.[50]

The military list grew from 502 names in 1841 to 753 during the rebellion of 1846–1847, then to 2,144 receiving no more than one-third pay or invalid's pension in 1857 near the end of the Monágas regime.[51] In 1880 the government required all officers to present proof of their commissions and by 1883 about 600 had been entered on the military list, which was published fairly regularly thereafter as part of the annual report of the Minister of War and Navy. In 1887 the military list had grown to 1,237. It was slightly longer in 1889, and shot up to 10,168 by 1894. The military list in 1897 had 12,529 names of whom only 595 were on active duty. There were at the same time 33 generals-in-chief and 1,496 generals. Thereafter the number declined as the men of the Western Andes, the Andinos, advanced to domination.

José Ladislao Andara asserted that the title of general was so common that it was "a synonym for señor, and there are as a consequence innumerable aspirations to supreme power, since a general is a caudillo, actual or in gestation." [52] A decade earlier Andres J. Vigas had observed that Dr. Vicente Coronado was called "General, perhaps because his name is so well-known that it is natural that he be attributed the rank that all Venezuelans hold in the militia." [53]

It is no wonder, then, that all but the highest military commissions lost their utility as rewards for public service, and even their luster was dimmed. The military commission under such circumstances was a disguise for political pensions and an indicator of political value, of what the Brazilians call *pistolao*. Gradual formation of a new military organization led by career officers to serve society in a professional way after 1890 [54] would facilitate eventually the attack of the national caudillo on the militia as he sought to provide public order and stability. Elimination of the militia, the auxiliary of caudillism, was a thirty-year process, eased by the increasing effectiveness of the army which gained mastery over the militia in the 1902–1903 rebellion and never again lost it.[55] Abolition of the militia ended the main institutional means for systematizing the personal alliance structure of caudillism. It meant the end of diffused violence and of caudillism. The militia in the process of its elimination was superseded by the several levels of public office. A bureaucracy of patronage replaced the officer corps of the militia as the main device to rationalize the personal political alliances of caciquismo. The machete and the gun, the noisy violence of caudillo and campesino, gave way to the more selective, individualized, silent violence of abusive use of legal action backed up by a professional army.

Conversion of caudillos into caciques was getting under way by the time Gómez replaced Cipriano Castro. Juan Vicente would devote a decade to the task. The Provisional President of the State of Sucre, an outsider from Guayana, reported in November 1909 that he had quieted the State's caudillos, had restored order in administration, and had balanced the budget. The problems of Sucre had not been resolved, but were being brought within manageable size:

Each chief of party or group has a district, and in accord with the majority and the law each has organized his [area] as he considered best without the slightest intervention from the government of the State. . . .

General Arcos and his group have a district, Morales has another, Córdova another, Pancho Vásquez another, Velásquez-Herrera another. Mariño District is divided, half for the friends of P. Ducharme, and half for the group opposed to the Ducharmes, the Gutiérrez Group.

I have appointed to all State offices Cumaneses from all parties without distinction of party labels. I have acted as their 'bond of union' and of supply. . . . Naturally with a little State so small and so poor divided among so many chiefs it is not possible perfectly to satisfy all their hopes, to say nothing of their pretensions. In Barcelona there are no more than two parties, but here there are eight.

The same official, devoted to the patriotic themes of work, prosperity, and progress, was sorely disappointed in caudillos who thought only of their personal interest. Satisfaction of their demands in a minimal manner had imposed on him a burden of personal indebtedness. But he could assure the president of Venezuela that all caudillos of following "with but a single *insignificant exception,* have had and have participation in state jobs." [56]

The despotic phase of caudillism was obviously affected or influenced in its development by economic growth, population increase, and greater political sophistication. There was no intellectual force or institution left after the defeat of the Church by Guzmán Blanco to check the growth of despotism, of intellectual abasement before power. The caudillo become despot found a base for strength in independent government income from oil and in a disciplined professionally-led armed force which was the creature of the regime.

4 | ON THE OCCASIONS OF VIOLENCE

Many Venezuelan military leaders of the wars for independence had their start as guerrilla leaders, a role which they initially held as representatives of major families or as natural leaders who became dominant in some locality in the struggle for survival. Guerrilla units did not suddenly appear as new full-blown gangs of men devoted to the practice of violence after April 19, 1810, but their numbers would be greatly enlarged thereafter. In their earlier form they existed as cattle rustling and other outlaw units in the llanos. Cattle rustling began early in the eighteenth century when mavericking and other customary practices related to livestock as a *res nullius* were made illegal by the Cabildo of Caracas. Rustling and armed robbery developed as Caracas tried to enforce its ordinances.[1]

The Political and Military Commandant of Barinas reported in 1794 that

robberies of various houses in the campo had been frequent during the preceding year, committed by the Guamos Indians,
accompanied by other ill-living zambos and mulattoes who,
pursued for their grave crimes not only in this jurisdiction but
also in the neighboring provinces, live lawlessly under the protection of the Guamos. My greatest efforts, as is well known,
do not suffice to contain them since they are masters and highly
skilled in these immense mountains whence they come forth to
carry on their raids with the certainty of no opposition from the
few Spanish vecinos that could do so; and when I am informed
of the fact so I can act more effectively, they are already back
in their peaks and rocks where they have no fixed base, since
the length of more than fifty leagues of the Mountain of Mas-
parro enables them to change their base, rendering useless the
measures that I have taken so many times to capture them.[2]

Alexander von Humboldt and his party preferred not to
travel by day in the Venezuelan llanos in 1800 since the
llanos were "infested . . . by thieves that murdered . . .
the whites who fell into their hands." He also commented
that "nothing is worse than the administration of justice in
these overseas colonies. Everywhere we find the prisons full
of evildoers, whose sentence was pronounced only after
seven or eight years of delay." Of these prisoners about a
third escaped to live in any way they could in the llanos.[3]
At the time Humboldt was traveling in Venezuela the new
Captain General, Guevara Vasconcelos, was attempting to
improve the administration of justice. The poor condition
of the courts was due in great part to the appointment of
men of no standing in the localities as *tenientes de justicia*.
Guevara replaced many of them with leading local citizens.[4]

A crisis in public order existed in the llanos in 1810 when
the war for independence began. There were indications
that the lawless individuals and small bands were coalescing

into larger units, interfering with the normal operation of the Venezuelan economy.[5] Venezuela's famed José Antonio Páez while driving a herd by way of Banco Largo in mid-1809 encountered a slave revolt at Las Huerfanitas. He assisted the slaves, took over leadership, and organized a force of 350 men, most of them llaneros. Five days later he attacked the town of Calabozo with 600 men and his force was driven off. A faithful group of two hundred llaneros went with him to the Llanos of Apure. Nine months later, early in 1810, he was in the region of Portuguesa with two thousand lancers. Many other guerrilla units were formed during these months and engaged in a variety of lawless activities.[6]

Bolívar succeeded in dominating the major guerrilla leaders during the course of the war, and as long as the campaigning lasted the staff and command standards he taught them made the guerrilla leaders and their men an effective fighting force.[7] "After Carabobo all the world expected to collect its share: all dreamed of wealth and above all desired command. The ten years of campaigns had hardened men and accustomed officers to be caciques, to be absolute masters and to be obeyed by an unthinking herd as in the savage epoch of the war to the death." [8] Violence practiced to obtain the means of warfare continued as a political technique after the active phase of campaigning had ended, and for a century the caudillos served to "focus the barbarous will of men." [9]

Neither the army nor the militia (auxiliary or civic) was being used to maintain public order. Guerrillas were active in some districts of the Province of Caracas at the end of 1824. The situation was not helped by the conflict between General Páez and the Intendant of the Department of Vene-

zuela, General Escalona. The problem was further complicated by inability of the government of Colombia to obtain
enough revenue to meet its obligations. Civil and military
officials suffered delays in pay, although the civil list took
second place to the military in receiving pay. A general
decay of authority and a spirit of insubordination in the
towns also made it possible for a growing number of people
to escape taxation. During the long political crisis which
rose in 1825 and receded in 1827 troops were deserting,
towns were reassuming their sovereign rights, and the Valencia Insurrection (the *Cosiata*) in Venezuela in April 1826
nearly fractured the Republic of Colombia. Crime was
rampant.[10] Insecurity of life and property was such that
hacendados in the Province of Caracas lobbied through a
local decree in 1827 authorizing and organizing a patrol system at the expense of rural producers. Patrons were to arrest
thieves, buyers of stolen goods, escaped slaves, and the
vagrant unemployed. Other parts of Venezuela adopted the
organization.[11]

The urgency of the situation was stated by José Rafael
Revenga, Secretary General of Bolívar, in his report to congress in 1827: "The state of [Venezuela], the resistance
made on the one hand by those that call themselves friends
of government, the unrest and new sedition of those very
people lately relieved of the fratricidal dagger, dispersion
of the armed forces, until recently in garrison, in various
places, the greater dispersion of arms, and the unease with
which these symptoms are everywhere viewed, make the
Eastern Departments a vast battlefield." Bolívar's firm hand
and insistence on ending impunity through prompt justice
by means of new courts, calmed the situation in 1827. He
also ordered the repossession of government arms as well as

limitations on the sale of arms.[12] It was fleeting at best, because Bolívar, confronted by the Cosiata and influenced by his special feeling for Venezuela, rewarded the rebels of the Cosiata. He gave them control of the Venezuelan area, subject only to his personal authority as president of Colombia. Venezuela thus enjoyed special status within Colombia, which eventually simplified and eased the whole process of secession from Colombia. Páez as Jefe Superior Militar y Civil of Venezuela dealt with the problem of rebellious guerrilla activity and resolved it in much the same way that Bolívar had used in dealing with him and his associates. Páez found that, as in his own case, such settlements did not satisfy the guerrilla leaders, who continued their activities.[13]

Although the years from 1830 to 1846 are reputed a period of order, stability, and financial responsibility,[14] guerrilla groups continued to exist: "Parties of armed men infested the empty lands and assaulted the ranches and towns of the llanos as in colonial times. Their trials and sentences were reported in the Gaceta de Venezuela. . . . Members of these gangs were not only llaneros (zambos and mulattoes), but many were workers, artisans, displaced farmers, besides a multitude of slaves and manumitted persons." [15] A biographer of the noted guerrillero leader Matías Salazar has commented on the ephemeral or incidental nature of the episodes of armed activity. Thus, after the federalist cause won in the 1860's most of the chiefs went home to government jobs or to other private pursuits. Salazar went to Cojedes where he played the role of an agitator, demagogue, leading politician, and influential figure in the regional militia. In 1869 he organized another guerrilla force to help Antonio Guzmán Blanco to power in 1870.[16]

Páez was the maximum leader after 1830 on the basis of his unrivalled prestige among the llaneros, his military record, and his leadership in the secession of Venezuela. There was almost no element to oppose him. High society in Caracas and the provinces was badly thinned by the wars for independence and it longed for tranquillity. The llaneros inspired a degree of social panic on the basis of their past record, nor was a strong military force regarded as any better than the llaneros. Besides, an army was useless while the country was full of veterans to respond to the call of Páez.[17] Out of mutual need the old and the new orders of leadership were drawn together into a working alliance which lasted until 1846.

In the decade from 1825 to 1835 Páez speeded up the decline of the veteran officers of independence who had expected to be the dominant political force. Taking advantage of the Militia Law of Colombia he began in 1826 to build a militia organization. Upon secession from Colombia the process was augmented by open reliance on the militia for public order maintenance and by provision for a very reduced permanent force. Protest against secession and against the traits of the new government expressed in the Rebellion of 1831 led to the exile of a number of the most influential officers of independence fame. The outbreak of the War of the Reforms of 1835 confirmed the victory of the armed populace over a minuscule permanent force and an associated lengthy list of veteran officers of the war for independence.

The occasion for the military revolt of 1835 was the election of Dr. José María Vargas, the candidate of the anti-military civilians who represented the four C's of Venezuela: *café, caña, cacao,* and Caracas. Civilians were irritated by the role of Páez and his associates and they over-estimated the stability of republican institutions and the degree of popular esteem for the rule of law. Páez pliantly yielded to the pressure for the time being and was content to await events. The impact of the War of Reforms, the resignation of President Vargas, and the election of General Carlos Soublette, a *paecista,* in 1837 as vice president (presidential and vice presidential terms overlapped two years) assured the llanero chieftain control of the executive branch.[18]

Police Inspector Gregg of Surrey, England, who had served in Colombia as a lieutenant colonel and stayed through the 1820's interpreted the rebellion as a subtle maneuver of Páez to make himself indispensable as the personal guarantor of public peace. Gregg believed leaders of the rebellion were agents of Páez, that their defeat would enhance the republican image of Páez, a monarchist at heart, and enable him to check the ambitions of the oligarchy and the intellectuals to be free of all military-identified figures in the national government.[19] Clearly, the civilians preferred the cacique to the caudillo and his imminent violence. The contemporary Venezuelan historians, Baralt and Díaz, attributed the rebellion to a Caracan alliance of Bolivarian monarchists and of Democrats, a 1960's alliance of the far right and far left. In the provinces the alliance won support among military men aggrieved by loss of fuero, boredom, and their laborious poverty.[20]

The Governor of Trinidad reported that military ambition was the cause of the revolt. The Libertadores felt cheated of their rights by Páez and his civilian associates, and sought to claim their individual shares of Venezuela.[21] On the whole, Trinidad's governor emphasized the thwarted

caciquismo of the Libertadores and their resort to praetori-
anism. They sought political office. None of the sources
examined attribute to the Bolivarians desire for an enlarged
and more professional army. They demanded full fuero and
the acknowledgement that Venezuela was their creation
and theirs to govern. It is equally clear that José Tadeo
Monágas, a Libertador, with his power rooted in his region
among his retainers, was the major profiteer among the
rebels of 1835–1836. He and his supporters, clearly able to
strain the resources of the government, won as the price of
peace not only an amnesty and security from any property
loss, but also all they had gained in property and military
rank assumed during the rebellion. Cabinet Minister Santos
Michelena tendered his resignation because of the settlement made between Páez and Monágas: "I am convinced
that confirmation of the military rank of the rebels of Barcelona that have twice betrayed the Republic approves
the impunity of the greatest of crimes: that said confirmation is opprobrious for Venezuela and dishonorable to its
loyal defenders, and that the impunity of those [rebels] and
the disgust of these [defenders] sooner or later will produce
new conspiracies and therefore new misfortunes for the
fatherland. . . ." [22]

By his successful conciliation of the Monágan sector of
the rebellion and the defeat of the Bolivarian sector in the
War of the Reform, Páez confirmed his personal authority
over the second administration of independent Venezuela
which had opened under Dr. Vargas. His victory was emphasized by the insistence of Vargas on resigning, which
brought Páez's collaborator Soublette to the presidency
upon his election as vice president in 1837 to succeed the
acting president whose term as vice president was ending.

Páez also cleared the way for a new generation of caudillos. It was clear that the government bargained with caudillos if they would deal and exiled officers if it could.[23] The new crop of caudillos embodied the growing resentment against the political system erected by Páez and the patriciate to ensure their dominance. The leaders and their guerrillas were triggered into action by the new Liberal Party whose emergence is tied to the second or anarchic phase of caudillism.

Ten years elapsed before the results of the War of the Reforms became evident. In that interval the first administration of Soublette (1837–1839) and the second of Páez (1839–1843) were the high point of conservative patrician or gamonal-cum-cacique influence, the element commonly considered a responsible self-centered republican elite by Venezuelan historians.[24] The non-military flavor has been described by Sir Robert Ker-Porter who reported the dullness and discontent of the congressmen at the 1839 inauguration of Páez who "is *too great* and *too particularly good* for them. . . . The business was a dull civil one—not a single uniform to enliven its look. . . ."[25]

Denial of public office to veteran officers of the army of independence, the unyielding grip of Páez and his entourage on public office and policy, the unsuccessful patrician effort to win political independence from Páez, and the perennial discontent of the ambitious and the intellectual had two profound results. After the dissolution of Gran Colombia "Páez witnessed the consolidation of a revolutionary group of almost all the military [Bolivarians] of Colombia, his imitators and some of his enemies." Because of defeat in 1831 and 1835, "Bolivarianism passed through a dismemberment that virtually destroyed it. . . ."[26] As this came to pass the Liberal Party began to emerge as a focus for all opposition and began regular existence in 1840. The effect of these two developments was to simplify the political situation: the prestige of Páez versus the opposition. Anarchic caudillism was at hand. It should be remembered, however, that the outgoing Soublette Administration in its handling of the elections of 1846 provided the excuse for its opponents to have recourse to the right of insurrection. Thereafter the Liberals blamed the Conservative patriciate, which they called an oligarchy, for the plague of civil violence after 1846.[27]

The Liberal position was supported by British Minister Bedford Wilson. He reported in 1846 that the balloting for electors had been peaceful, despite the fact that "the party which since the year 1830 has been in the possession of political ascendancy and power, in order to prolong that possession has endeavoured by every possible means, including the agitation of that most dangerous of all questions in Venezuela, namely, that of castes, to incite and provoke their opponents into a violation of the public peace, thereby affording a plea for calling in the aid of the Military Force and for effectually crushing their political opponents, under the semblance of upholding the Constitution and the Laws." [28]

The opening stage of a caudillesque assault on power has been described in simplified terms in a *La Religión* (Caracas) editorial of October 12, 1959:

Venezuelans are accustomed to the "revolutionary" uprisings called in criollo slang a "leap from the woods" or assault in which an unquiet señor, a rancher or owner of a coffee, cacao, or other agricultural hacienda, "gave the cry" on his property and took to the bush accompanied by 400 peons, armed with chopping machetes or even with ancient blunderbusses.

On beginning the campaign, our chief labelled himself with little ceremony or protocol general of the movement and named his friends and relatives colonels. Thus the undisciplined phalanx went from brush patch to brush patch, from village to village, eating stolen beef, robbing chicken yards, and enrolling any campesinos encountered into its ranks.

Succeeding phases are described in the *Gaceta de Venezuela* in its September 13, 1846, issue which reported that 150 men of the region of Güigüe and Magdaleno had entered Güigüe shouting *vivas* to Antonio Leocadio Guzmán and to Free Venezuela! They proclaimed "Death to the oligarchs!" The faction occupied the town, swarmed into the saloons, shot up the town, stole all the horses in the vicinity, recruited more members, and killed a few oligarchs. Francisco Rangel, known as El Indio, had "named himself colonel and Santos Rodríguez captain" of the force. Rangel was obviously more modest than many of his counterparts of a later day.

The occasion for the formation of the Rangel guerrilla was the election of 1846. Just as the more famed Zamora, Rangel had rebelled against local election abuses.[29] Páez and his partners in the patriciate were hard pressed to continue their control of government as the elections of 1846 approached. The electors chose 8,798 electors whose commitments were split among five candidates, none of whom had a majority. Only 342 of the electors actually convened and they divided their votes between two Libertadores, Generals Salom and José Tadeo Monágas. Salom's majority was not the necessary two-thirds, so congress completed the election. Under the influence of Páez, congress chose Monágas[30] despite his turbulent record in the rebellions of 1831 and 1835. According to the British Minister, Monágas

is a respectable, well-meaning, uneducated man, and is not remarkable for natural abilities; however, his deficiency in these
latter respects are all but confessedly the circumstances that in-
duced the party designated as the Oligarchy, which since 1830
has obtained the political ascendancy and power, to raise him
to the presidency, in the expectation of finding in him a pliant
instrument, notwithstanding his political sympathies and associates hitherto have been opposed to their domination.

Present appearances justify the correctness of this calcula-
tion; nevertheless, as cunning and distrust are the most prominent features of the Venezuelan character and more especially
of the 'llaneros' or natives of the plains, it would be hazardous
to offer any prediction as to the policy likely to be pursued,
eventually, by General Monágas.[31]

Neither abusive electoral procedures nor the candidacy of
Monágas resolved the problems confronting the patriciate.
The discontented left for the hills to begin a guerrilla attack
on local and national government.

Behind the uprising lay several years of increasing agricultural depression, the ruin of financially over-extended
farmers and hacendados whom the high coffee prices of
1835–1840 had enticed into costly expansion.[32] Depression
brought into full force the terms of the law of April 10,
1834, protecting creditors in an unlimited manner. There
were numerous bankruptcies. Demand and agitation to set
a legal rate of interest undermined confidence at home and
abroad in Venezuelan credit and investments. Financial
alarm was heightened by an effort to promote the printing
of paper money and the borrowing of foreign funds for lend-
ing at six per cent.[33] An effort to amend the law on credit
failed because conferees representing the two houses of congress could not agree on common language for such a law.[34]
To these events add the effects of uninhibited Liberal Party

propaganda.[35] A Conservative's reaction to the rise of the Liberal Party, its propaganda, and the impact of its doctrines is provided by Aniceto Serrano who wrote:

With the doctrine of El Venezolano the harmony between the hacendados and their peons disappeared as well as the concord between the proprietors and their tenants, arousing these insatiable hopes of sudden fortunes, ambitions that could not easily be satisfied, and [claiming] rights they said were usurped by those who helped maintain order and justice. No purpose [is] at once easier and less dangerous to accomplish in a society that had been subordinated to the habits of obedience, of tutelage, and even of slavery for more than three hundred years (as Guzmán was saying) than that of confounding the beliefs of those simple men, their customs and the convictions of their souls, infusing in them the idea that rebellion against those leading them along the way of morality and work would improve their condition and the state of their families. They would acquire full right to the lands they rented [and] full possession and enjoyment of privileges and prerogatives usurped by their ill-disguised leaders, and even coming to possess aptitude to all the offices of honor and trust which the proclaimed legal equality opened up to them in the institutions of the land.[36]

Venezuela was beginning to feel the same onset of social turbulence which troubled the whole Western world at mid-nineteenth century. The reaction of that segment of the patriciate exercising political influence and of the business community was defensive. These groups for the most part looked to the "leading proprietors in the republic," Páez and Monágas, to dominate the conflict between civilization and barbarism and to prevent a general distribution of offices, lands, wealth, and women.[37]

Progressive decline of public order down to 1858 responded to the assaults on power. Monágas seized power assisted by the remaining Bolivarian officers to whom Páez had denied a political role. He was supported by a discontented element of the patriciate. The anarchic stage of caudillism had begun, and it was accompanied by a sharp decline in the socio-political level of the people. Monágas, his family, and his friends and supporters destroyed the pragmatic devices developed by Páez and his oligarchy to impose a civilian rule of law on Venezuela. The task was not too difficult for Monágas since the major stabilizing influence in the state had been the personality of Páez. The evidence of decaying public order was brought sharply to public attention by the assault on congress, January 24, 1848, by the Caracan mob and militia at the instigation of the Executive Branch. A British source related that the incident was devised to complete the overthrow of the oligarchy and its representatives in congress and the judiciary at the very moment in which an effort to impeach the president was viewed as the only means to return the oligarchy to control of government.[38]

The decay of the patriciate was clear as was its replacement by "heterogeneous groups produced by the already inevitable social revolution." [39] These heterogeneous groups plundered the country. As the Monagan era approached its end, domestic debt was sharply increased by agiotismo, no payments were being made on the foreign debt, and the directors of the Banco de Accionistas which served the treasury flooded the country with paper and shipped the metal currency abroad. Impunity reigned as crime in and out of government went unpunished. "The struggle between Civilization and Barbarism was at hand." [40]

From 1858 on the caudillos with their guerrillas attacked power to conquer it, giving to society the appearance of decomposition.[41] In 1858 guerrilla units were common in Guárico, Portuguesa, and Barinas. All proclaimed themselves Liberal, most were headed by men sporting military titles, and most of them joined together under the leadership of a man who claimed no military title, Carlos J. Colón Fuentes,[42] but control of the national government was first held by General Julian Castro, Governor of the Province of Carabobo. As the Castro regime came under attack, United States Chargé Turpin commented on "the most unaccountable apathy and inactivity," among Castro's subordinates despite his orders.[43] Government military movements against the rebels scarcely merited the name. Turpin also noted that the true motives of the guerrillas were revenge and plunder, but that they gave their activities a political label to gain the immunity from capital punishment accorded political crimes.[44] Castro, in the face of deliberate inactivity sponsored among his subordinates by his own father-in-law, General Laurencio Silva, tried to switch sides by changing his Conservative cabinet for a Liberal one, by granting amnesty, and by giving Liberals control of government in exchange for one of the top posts in government. The Liberals turned down the offer, and Castro resigned on August 1, 1859.[45] A succession of constitutionally based replacements tried to resolve the situation. During this period, Turpin cited as a rule of thumb among the revolutionary guerrilla forces "all who are not for us are against us," and the latter were invariably plundered and assassinated.[46]

Rebel activities were successful until the most effective rebel field commander, Ezequiel Zamora, was killed. Subsequent rebel losses did not mean, however, that government was able to dominate the opposition whose forces had broken up into marauding gangs. By October 1860 the dead of such violence in two years were estimated at fifteen to twenty thousand.[47] The struggle between government and the guerrilla bands proclaiming the federalist system of government continued. As late as October 8, 1862, the United States Chargé reported there was no "concentrated organized opposition nor any recognized leadership or head of what opposition there is." [48] The opposing sides, unable to dominate each other in the field, negotiated a settlement. Financial exhaustion was probably the factor which accounted for the government's conclusion of a peace which was a federalist victory. The leading Federalist figures, Generals Juan Falcón and Antonio Guzmán Blanco, became the heads of government.[49] Until the accession of Guzmán Blanco to power in 1870 the nation continued in anarchy as a host of caudillos with their guerrillas struggled to seize and hold power at the several levels of government. Of this difficult era, Cecilio Acosta (1818–1881) has observed that ambition made a chief of "anyone who put together a group of volunteers whom he led in slaughter and looting, achieving political power through the exaltation of the uneducated classes." [50] Powerful as Guzmán Blanco was, he was unable to repress the major manifestations of caudillism for longer than the first seven of his twenty years of predominance.

According to Level de Goda the "triumph of the Federal Revolution . . . brought to the top of society and government a part of the barbarous element of Venezuela . . . which has weighed heavily in national destiny; and, dominating the localities and even the capital, it was natural that misgovernment, disorder, and anarchy should follow. . . . From this unfortunate period dates the plague of generals. . . . War became endemic in different localities. . . .

Each of the Federal States . . . was governed with few exceptions by a kind of cacique." [51] These views contrast sharply to those held in 1864 when the establishment of the federal system was hailed by a leading Liberal publicist as the advent of local autonomy and of the rule of law. The rule of law was equated to the sovereign role of public opinion. The publicist celebrated the end of the era in which politics and government reflected the pervading dominance of Caracas and during which local affairs went well if a district leader or officials were on good terms with authority in Caracas.[52] The Blue Revolution of 1868 was attacked by *El Federalista* on the grounds that "some political pedants believe that Venezuela cannot be governed except by them: some hundreds of *parasites* with military titles and a reputation as bonny men, and a certain number of Blues that sought in the Revolution of June nothing more than a reinstatement of their commissions and powers in order to resume living without working." [53]

Guzmán Blanco, who had replaced Falcón as the chief of the Federalists, unseated the Blues in 1870 and imposed his will on the country. His very executive measures were aided by the fact that "constitutional rights being neither prized nor even thought of by the great bulk of the population . . . ," he could attempt the repossession of arms and disband the army. "The multitude of ignorant dissolute individuals utterly unfit for any useful employment in the sphere in which they were born, who overrun the country, possessed of a General's commission and nothing in the world besides, will be deprived of the means of promoting anarchy, kidnaping the honest labourer, or devastating estancias; for a time at least, whilst their chance, at least for the present, of acquiring sufficient prominence to be able to obtain from the cautious speculators of the Island of Curaçao, sufficient War Material for any wider development of their subversive plans will be much diminished." The same source observed that the public did not believe in a lasting peace and viewed Guzmán Blanco's effort at agricultural development as a temporary phase for pecuniary gain.[54]

Rebellions for limited objectives were common in the period after 1870. The following examples are typical. Dr. Santiago Briceño and General Rosendo Medina organized a local revolution in 1878. Leaders of the local groups in the uprising included men who did not assert any military rank. In all some 5,000 men made rendezvous to overthrow a state government.[55] Rebels from all elements of society took part in the revolution of 1886 against the sectional chief of Táchira, General Espíritu Santo Morales. The revolt was caused by the misconduct of public officials whom Morales would not check because he was too easy with his friends and supporters.[56] A course of events such as the following would lead eventually to an uprising. In 1897 after all the militia units in Táchira were ordered into San Cristóbal, the commanding officer warned the pro-Cipriano Castro militia officers to leave lest they be arrested. Santiago Briceño Ayestarán left his unit and on his way out of town met a friend at the head of his unit from the district of Tariba. Briceño advised him of the situation. The friend ordered his second in command to lead the unit back to Tariba to report to his brother for dismissal from duty status. The unit commander sent his brother instructions to hide the weapons in a secure place, and then went into exile with the Briceños.[57]

Election abuses provided the occasion for the civil conflict of 1898. President Joaquín Crespo in anticipation of trouble again had recourse to the division of the country into five military regions, the system first devised by Guzmán Blanco. Defeated candidate José María Hernández, El Mocho, left Caracas to begin a rebellion against the new administration of President Andrade. He contacted General Evaristo Lima, a distinguished political figure and hacendado, and they set the date for March 2, 1898. Lima's finca named Queipa was headquarters for the rebellion. Friends were contacted and given the rendezvous date. As people began to arrive the news got out and the rebellion was advanced a day in time. The uprising began with forty-five men who left Queipa to meet other groups expected to arrive March 2. By the evening of March 2 the force numbered two hundred. Other sympathizers organized groups and rebelled, some under Conservative leaders of renown, others under the leadership of farmers and merchants, including a landowner whose major-domo was a general.[58] Among the rebels General Cipriano Castro rose to victory, toppling the Andrade Administration. The disorder was attended and followed by large scale robbery and rustling operations, despite Castro's slogan of "New Men, New Ideas, and New Methods," [59] because "these local military chieftains that come to the surface . . . are in many cases practically amenable to no established central authority." [60] Even Castro was driven to forced loans. He jailed the bankers until they came across with the necessary funds. Among those so treated was banker Manuel Matos, Minister of Finance of ousted President Andrade. Matos, one of Venezuela's wealthiest men, determined to overthrow Castro.[61] He, too, was called general. His failure to remove Castro helped rivet Andino control on Venezuela.

5 | ON SOME CAUDILLOS

The records of some of these commissioned caudillos have been revealed in a number of biographies and memoirs. An examination of their lives serves only to underline the political and violent—but not professional military—careers of the caudillos of the nineteenth century. Their bearing of arms, their appropriation of military titles, and the magnitude of their violence filled the eye. Thus Ramón Escobar Salom has noted the relative paucity of data on civilian figures not linked with violence in the independence era "compared with the quantity that exists on some caudillos of independence who joined it not out of republican idealism nor strictly constructive purpose, but because the adventure stirred their vital urges and the warrior's career offered them an active form of vagabondage. . . . These caudillos, emergent from the formless, barbarous and destructive guerrilla, have supplied for a long time the symbols of a nation."[1]

The patriciate feared the numerous officers who were unable to satisfy their desire for wealth or lacked the education and the desire for work, who wanted "to be perpetuated or placed in command in order not to feel so intensely the need to renounce the free life on campaign." The famed General Antonio Sucre considered the citizens in Venezuela in 1830 dominated and oppressed by a military class possessed by a capricious personalism.[2] The capricious personalism and the military titles continued, the quasi-professionals of the wars for independence did not.

Ezequiel Zamora, born in 1817, had an uneventful youth until at age 18 he took a trip to Guárico with a lawyer relative. There he made his first cattle deal. Until 1846 he was a merchant, and operated out of a number of towns until he settled in Villa de Cura. There he joined the Liberal Party early in the 1840's and became its local leader. Commissioned a lieutenant in 1844 by the jefe político of his district, he served in the militia in 1844–1845. Zamora became a Liberal candidate for office in the 1846 elections. A quarrel with an election judge who was disqualifying Liberal ballots led to Zamora's arrest. When released, he sold his store, paid his debts, organized a guerrilla force, and joined the uprisings then developing. He quickly earned the respect of the men of the countryside but was captured in 1847. Sentenced to death, he escaped in January, 1848, and joined Monágas who had turned against the men who brought him to the presidency and aligned himself with the Liberals. Zamora was assigned the duty of forming a battalion in Villa de Cura and of pursuing his erstwhile captors.

Promoted to general in 1854, he married the sister of General Falcón in 1856. He abandoned his new career of training militia units for the government and went into farming in the Coro area. General Julian Castro seized the government in 1858, persecuted the Liberals, and Zamora and Falcón went into exile after organizing the Federal Movement. They soon returned to initiate the long social conflict known as the Federal War, 1859–1864, during which Zamora died.[3]

Juan C. Falcón, famed leader of the Federalist armies in the great conflict, was born in the province of Coro in 1820 to a family of prominent landowners. His first revolutionary action occurred in 1848 against the Monágas regime. At the time he held the grade of major, an elective post in the militia. Such grades were the prerogative of citizens of major influence in a locality, and Falcón held such a position in the Serranías of San Luis and Cabure. Reconciled after the rebellion, he served from 1849 to 1853 at Maracaibo, and returned to Coro in 1853 as commandant of arms of the province with the rank of colonel. After the campaigns of 1854 he was promoted to general of division, and in 1857 was given command of the Barquisimeto garrison. Prior to Monágas's resignation in March 1858, the president had ordered Falcón to disarm and dismiss the forces under his command. General Julian Castro who had toppled the Monágas regime censured the conduct of Falcón. The latter went into exile in Curaçao. There with the aid of Ezequiel Zamora he organized the Federalist invasion. There, too, he persuaded Antonio Guzmán Blanco, talented son of the able politician Antonio Leocadio Guzmán, to join his force. Falcón's success as a leader of revolution was not matched by administrative skill, political understanding, nor abiding love for public office. His subordinates, principally Guzmán Blanco, handled affairs, but incapacity at the head meant that the caudillos were not dominated, that the country continued in disorder. The disaster of the Falcón administration was ended by the ouster of President Falcón in 1868 from an office he seldom actually filled. He died late in April 1870.[4]

Matías Salazar was a brilliant undisciplined caudillo, ill-advised in his fatal last adventure. During his lifetime he was peddler, clerk, bullfighter, bandit, teacher, farmer, carpenter, stockman, general, state president, and Second Designate to the Presidency of Venezuela. Born in 1828, he was on his own by the time he reached twenty years of age. At thirty he began his political career in the Federal War as a second lieutenant in the Federalist forces. Willful though he was, he became a successful leader of guerrilla units and of the more formally organized units that took shape during the civil war. The anti-Federal Blue Revolution brought the Monágas family back to power briefly at the end of the 1860s. As one of several regional caudillos whose forces comprised the aggregation supporting Federalism and Guzmán Blanco, Salazar was the dominant figure in the fighting in central Venezuela to displace Monágas. He emerged as the number three man in a Venezuela headed by Provisional President Antonio Guzmán Blanco. Almost immediately he distrusted Guzmán Blanco's upper class tastes and took to plotting. Foiled in his effort to kill the president Salazar traveled to the United States, and then returned to Venezuela via Colombia early in 1872 to lead an unsuccessful rebellion. Captured in May of that year, he was tried by a military court of twenty-three generals-in-chief, convicted, and executed.[5]

Some men were secretaries first and then caudillos. General Francisco Tosta García early in his career entered into the service of General Quintana as a lieutenant in 1870. Quintana did not offer a very brilliant future since he preferred to stay home and take care of his hacienda. Tosta as a young Liberal had attracted the displeasure of the briefly revived Monagan regime (1868–1870) and had to leave Caracas. Quintana sent Tosta with a message to General Desiderio Escobar. Escobar and all his force were illiterate, so Escobar retained Tosta as his secretary and within a few days made him second in command of the army. Tosta commanded a section of it in the capture of Caracas in 1870 and came out of the campaign a general at the age of twenty-four.[6]

Most successful of all secretaries, however, was Antonio Guzmán Blanco, who was persuaded in Curaçao to join the forces being organized by General Falcón to invade Venezuela in 1859. Guzmán Blanco with the rank of major and of secretary to General Falcón became editor of the army newspaper. He parlayed the job into Venezuela's largest fortune of his time and into nearly twenty years of political predominance over the nation.[7] He also unmistakably used nationalism as a political instrument. Thus in 1873 the right of the foreigner to call on his government for assistance was limited by law, and the Venezuelan government denied any responsibility for damages, seizures, and injuries not caused by its officials in line of duty. Four years later, as he prepared to leave office, he declared that he had "restored the dignity of the country . . . before the foreigner."[8]

General Manuel Modesto Gallegos, teacher, clerk, trader, and politician, went into politics when he met General Joaquín Crespo at a social function in October 1874 at the home of a storekeeper, General Tomás Hernández, who employed Gallegos as a cotton buyer and bookkeeper. Crespo invited him to join his staff on campaign. By the end of the campaign in 1875 Gallegos was a major. The following four years he made his living as a peddler traveling between Caracas and Puerto Cabello, and in 1880 entered political office as a customs official. He was subsequently governor of a federal territory.[9]

General Ramón Guerra, born in 1843 in the State of Miranda, possessed a scant education, but his natural mathematical talents formed the basis for his success in commerce and in political conflict. At sixteen he was a sergeant in the militia and became a cavalry officer under Páez. In 1864 he served as major-domo to a rancher, took part in the Blue Revolution of 1868, and then returned to ranching. He was generally opposed to the policies of Guzmán Blanco and found it advisable in 1872 to move to Apure. There he avoided government harassment by helping to defeat the Salazar rebellion, and then resumed his ranching and farming activities. He expanded into merchandising, and assisted in the return of Guzmán Blanco to power in 1879. He was recalled again from his business activities to assist in the repression of guerrilla groups in 1881. Always a lukewarm supporter of Guzmán Blanco, Guerra fell under suspicion and was imprisoned in 1882. Upon his release in ill health in 1886 he found his wife gravely ill and his properties in ruin. He had rebuilt his fortune by 1892, and in that year joined Crespo's revolution as a protest against the resumption of government harassment. As government forces approached his home town on April 3, 1892, Guerra rallied a force of five hundred men armed with clubs, machetes, and hunting guns. He led it off for training, avoiding immediate combat.

On April 6 he was joined by three more generals and in the following days another nine generals drifted in. Guerra led his growing force from success to success. He served the Crespo Administration in the constitutional assembly, filled the post of Minister of War and Navy, and was a member of the Grand Military Council.[10] In the rebellion against the Andrade Administration in 1899, Guerra, as provisional president of the State of Guárico, took to the field in rebellion. With government approval the businessmen of Caracas sent an agent to buy Guerra's support of the government. Guerra demanded double the one hundred thousand gold dollars they offered plus payment of his fighting expenses and the right to name the president of Guárico. No agreement was reached, and Guerra was subsequently defeated in battle.[11]

Andres J. Vigas published a series of profiles or thumbnail sketches of prominent political figures in congress and the administration from 1889 to 1891. Of those men with military titles he stated that General Ovidio M. Abreu was head of government in the State of Zamora for eighteen years; General José Onope Agullera was secretary to the president and a cabinet politician; General Juan Bautista Araujo was Conservative caudillo of Los Andes for many years and, by virtue of a conciliatory appointment by Guzmán Blanco in 1881, he was one of the first military delegates; General Jesús M. Ariesteguieta was a kinetic politician who served in many militia posts; General Diego Arreaza Monágas was a cattle rancher and almost-pacifist with but one and a half campaigns to his credit; General Ramón Ayala was an indomitable but long inactive warrior; General Francisco Batalla, a rich but honorable official notable for his brilliant attire, was President of the State of Zamora; General Manuel

María Bermúdez was poet, gourmet, generous, wordy, occasional secretary to Guzmán Blanco, Supreme Court Justice, and so poor a conspirator he had given up conspiring; Generals Avelino Briceño and Cipriano Urdaneta had excellent ancestry; General José I. Casañas was merchant and farmer, intensely regional in his interests, Minister of Interior, and brother of the President of the State of Bermúdez; General Rafael Carabaño was a good llanero and soldier; General Santos Carrera was a frank, conciliatory man of his word, a hardworking landowner in Oriente, who so cherished his prestige that he made every "effort that outside groups and even the national ones that sometimes sent agents there associated themeslves with him because of the confidence that his word inspires"; General Joaquín Crespo was ex-president, llanero, austere, and generous to his many friends in whom he suffered many disappointments; General R. Fonseca, whose political personality had evaporated some time ago and then returned by way of the bottle, had changed his occupation to cacao grower and was known as a laborious, generous, honorable llanero; General José María García Gómez was affable, popular, and a devoted dancer; Colonel Rómulo Guardia was a reporter in 1876, held political offices under Guzmán Blanco until he broke with him, and then returned to the press as director of the newspaper *La Libertad;* General Carlos Herrera headed a gang of demagogues in Cumaná, but was at heart an over-laborious farmer who had fought one field action which he lost—"another field action of his militia life comes to mind, and it is that when Benito Leocadio Guzmân went to Cumaná, he and his *muchachos* organized a riot and they put a bullet in his leg. . . . When he rose in support of General Crespo, he had to spend the three months the war lasted bush jumping in the eastern region . . ."; General José Angel Hernández Ron was a wealthy cattle dealer in eastern Guárico; General Manuel María Iturbe was "as a fiery Liberal a soldier before all else," and rose from non-commissioned rank to General of Division in the Federal War; General Jacinto Lara was polished, intellectual, consequent, and proud of his name; General Andrés Aurelio Level was statistically minded, grave, educated, courteous, a writer, and a census taker; General Domingo Monágas was always in financial difficulties because he was such a poor businessman, and he was an equally poor politician; and General Luis Sagarzu, who "is no general nor is he doctor; nevertheless they call him general who are nothing or who believe he ought to be one of the two things in a land where the general run of doctors are unlearned, and the unlearned in their majority are generals." [12]

José María Hernández, El Mocho, began his career rather early. He was left for dead at age seventeen on a battlefield in 1870. Thereafter he led a rootless wandering existence in the interior provinces of Venezuela and in the islands of the Antilles. In 1887 he returned to Venezuela for good. He became a gold miner in the new field of Yuruay where he entered local politics and led a rebellion to unseat the territorial chief. By 1892 he had taken over the state of Bolívar and begun his career in congress. He visited the United States where he became embroiled in a lawsuit over a contract he had cancelled while president of the State of Bolívar. His ambition led him to compete for the presidency in 1897. Hernández began his campaign with two Bolívares in his pocket and never wanted. Although he was enormously popular, fraudulent elections deprived him of victory. According to an election song:

Hernández had the masses	m*a*sas
Andrade had the election boards	m*e*sas
Rojas Paúl had the clergy	m*i*sas
Tosta García had the girls	m*o*sas
and Arismendi Brito had the muses	m*u*sas

Hernández organized a rebellion as a protest against repression of his supporters before and during the elections. The uprising began in March, developed slowly, gained momentum, but resulted in the rise of Cipriano Castro and the Andinos to national power.[13]

Colonel Pedro García Gil, garrison-trained career (1901–1945) military officer who never held a political post nor took part in a coup d'état, wrote that the Liberating Revolution of 1901 spread throughout Venezuela because of the social and political prestige of its banker-leader General Manuel A. Matos and of the regional chiefs who supported him. All regional chiefs held the title of general as did the four chiefs of staff of the revolutionary army. Colonel García Gil also noted the customary pre-Gómez practice of incorporating the troops of the defeated forces into the units of the victor.[14]

General Santiago Briceño Ayestarán, teacher, surveyor, merchant, publisher, commodity dealer, went into politics because of oppression at the hands of a caudillo. National caudillos in cleaning out the opposition ruined many opponents and bankrupted many Venezuelan merchants whose firms passed into the hands of their European creditors.[15] Such was the experience of Briceño Ayestarán. He joined the Cipriano Castro movement in 1898 and was named Chief of Uprising (*jefe de alzamiento*) in his home district of Táchira. Promoted to general in 1899 and to Supreme

Court Justice in 1900, he also served as Jefe Civil y Militar of Cumaná and of Sucre where he successfully reconciled the chiefs of the local parties to each other. As State President of Táchira in 1902 Briceño visited all the districts in the state to organize his following within the national Castro power structure. In a majority of the towns and localities he found generals of the proper Liberal association willing to acknowledge his leadership.[16] The value of such a personalist political structure paralleling the formal constitutional organization of the nation was its ability to make the government function and rapidly to mobilize people in political action. For example, General Francisco Linares Alcántara, caudillo of the region of Aragua for nearly two decades before he became president in 1877, could, through his subordinate caudillos, organize a fighting force of five to six thousand men in a week.[17] Consequently, the political significance of the elimination of the militia is difficult to overemphasize. It was the symbol of the active obligatory involvement of the citizen in the functioning of the social order. As a symbol it gave premier rank to muscular rather than to intellectual solutions to the conflicts of interest and ambition in the direction of government.

6 | THE MILITIA

The militia was intimately linked to the institution of caudillism in the nineteenth century. That development was the result of the erosion of the older political system and the continuing force of tradition or of established practice. The colonial militia had enlarged the role of the colonial mandón, even while that role was under attack from the crown through other government agencies. Command function in the colonial militia completed the multi-faceted influence of the patriciate as economic, social, and political leaders in Venezuelan society. The Venezuelan mandón, if he survived the war of independence as an active political force, became, as circumstances and talents determined, a gamonal, a cacique, or a caudillo, roles open to any element of society. In Venezuela the defeat of the mandón, that is of the patriciate, was mirrored in the changing character of the militia whose officer corps appears to have provided a degree of orderliness or of hierarchy for the caudillesque alliances headed up by the national caudillo.

Venezuelans had been subject to militia service for many generations. In the colonial era it was an obligation common to all parts of the Spanish empire, meeting the elemental needs of security in the absence of a standing army. In this respect the militia may properly be considered a continuation of the obligation of vassals to serve the king in return for land they held from him.[1] Venezuelan colonial documents refer to the calling up of the militia officers by civil authority. In 1720 the governor of the Province of Venezuela possessed the authority to appoint corregidores, tenientes, *cabos de guerra* for police functions, and captains and other militia officers.[2] During the reign of Charles III (1759–1788) the militia in the empire was converted from an informal rather *ad hoc* organization into regularly organized units drilled and trained in some degree by cadres of Spanish regulars on Sunday afternoons and holy days. In Venezuela it was expected to serve on coastal patrol duties as a guard against foreign attack, and did so function in repulsing the 1806 invasion attempted by Miranda. Some eight thousand men were mobilized.[3]

The reorganized militia system in Spain provided the pattern used in the national period in Venezuela. The Spanish militia had been revamped as a provincial militia by the Ordinance of January 31, 1734, and the system continued in force until 1846. Under the ordinance a regiment of provincial militia was composed of battalions divided into eight companies each. The companies were recruited in each *partido* among the better-off elements of the population, those less occupied in running haciendas, and, as much as possible, those without family obligations. Militia men were from twenty to forty years of age. Three professional officers were assigned to each regiment to discipline and train it. They were appointed and paid by the crown. The rest of the officers, from the commanding colonel down, were drawn from the wealthier landowners so that they could reinforce their military authority with their sociopolitical influence as proprietors over tenants, as masters over servants, as rich men over poor. The additional authority was apparently necessary to make up for the lack of instilled discipline of the trained soldier. Rural officers were paid only when their forces were mobilized. They were commissioned by the king from lists submitted by local authorities. These rural officers were also paid in terms of pride or distinction by use of the uniform and enjoyment of military fuero when on duty—after 1767 even when not on duty. Such a regiment cost only 8,000 reales a month to maintain. The local towns paid for uniforms out of their revenues and the crown supplied the guns. For about four million reales a year, Spain had in 1766 some forty-two provincial militia regiments, mostly on paper. Their veteran complements had been increased to fifteen men, the *compañía fija*, which included both noncommissioned officers and soldiers.[4] In 1767 nobles and hidalgos, their majordomos, valets, secretaries, and other employees essential to their dignity were exempt from militia service, as well as persons actually serving in public office. The mission of the militia was the maintenance of local public order in the absence of the army. Such was the system extended to the empire by Charles III in 1764.[5]

After 1769 the Reglamento for Cuban militia units became a basic guide for the rest of the empire. Gradually variations of it were developed in New Spain and in Nueva Granada, but the basic general pattern persisted. Militia units were made up of men aged sixteen to forty years recruited from town and fields for a ten year period. Exemptions from recruiting were roughly the same as those in Spain and were based on occupation and family need. Units were required to maintain their quality of personnel by basing selection on birth, good conduct, proper occupation, reputation, and sound evaluation of the capacity of the recruit, cadet, or officer. In selecting men and officers their public repute was of more importance than documents that could all too easily reflect local favoritism and influence. Men holding incompatible jobs were not to be recruited, and if a militiaman of any category accepted a degrading occupation, he was to be dismissed without rights or benefits. The units met each week for drill on Sundays for an hour if already trained and for two hours if not. A veteran cadre of instructors provided the training. Once a month the units were inspected. Militiamen could be excused from drill and monthly review in case of need, but everyone was obligated to be present at the annual assembly, attended by the Captain General of Venezuela or by the governor of the province.[6]

Every militiaman enjoyed fuero, both civil and criminal, and officers were to see to it that no one received its benefits without right. All militiamen were required to be respectful and cooperative towards civilian officials, who in turn were charged not to interfere in any way with the militia's activities but instead to assist its purposes. Thus local officials could not require any duty of militiamen except under urgent circumstances. The obligation to assist local authorities to enforce the law weighing on any vecino was limited to two hours for militiamen. Under their fuero militiamen could be assigned no obligatory public office nor guardianships without their consent, nor could their houses be used as billets nor their animals and equipment be requisitioned for troop use. They were exempted from a number of obligations to which other vecinos were subject, including special tax assessments (*repartimientos*), public work obligations, and payment of jailer's fees. White militia officers enjoyed the same status as regulars, while *pardos* and *morenos* were treated with esteem and enjoyed a position of dignity and respect in their respective classes. Under general practice applying to the Spanish provincial militia, single young men still under *patria potestad* could not enjoy benefits of fuero since they were not vecinos subject to public duties, but their parents possessed the military fuero in their stead which may partially explain the popularity of the militia in Venezuela. Fuero was the most effective device for checking the growing role of royal officials in the colonial power structure in Venezuela. Completion of twenty years' service in the militia entitled any person to lifetime fuero. While enrolled in the disciplined militia, any member possessed full fuero for his grade.[7]

Urban militia units continued to exist. They were organized on a company basis, generally without distinction of race and wore no special uniform. Governors of provinces or the Captain General sponsored such volunteer organizations and drafted the regulations determining their service and training. Prior to 1786 these units enjoyed a rather broad fuero for their members in criminal matters, but thereafter they possessed no fuero except when actually ordered to active duty.[8]

Development of the militia in Venezuela was hastened by

the Francisco de León rebellion of 1749–1753 against the Caracas Company, which in the years preceding the rebellion had maintained its own armed force, numbering from 600 to 1400 men. Local defense measures were much cheaper than movement of troops from Spain when some 3500 troops had been dispatched during the rebellion.[9] After 1757, colonial officials pushed militia organization, which became popular because of the advantages of fuero. Interest of royal officials in the Venezuelan provinces in development of a militia in the late 1750's was confirmed by a Real Cédula of December 5, 1760, which stated in part:

The King [has] taken satisfaction in the conduct of the natives and residents of that Province [of Caracas]. So that they may take part with the honor and interest they have shown in its defense as occasions occur, His Majesty has resolved that some companies of militia may be formed from their number, as many as you may decide on and consider convenient. All [units] set up may enjoy military fuero, not only the officers but also the sergeants, corporals, and soldiers that present themselves with uniforms and arms. In peace and in war they are to enjoy [fuero] in the same way as those other troops that serve for salary, holding exercises four times a month for better discipline and training, being supplied with the necessary powder from those stores. . . . This is to be publicized. . . .[10]

Among Venezuelans the mulatto element responded most readily to the attraction of fuero, uniform, and arms. By 1759 there were eight mulatto companies of militia. Mantuano interest developed on an effective scale after the royal cédula of 1760 which broadened the fuero and gave it a stronger legal basis. The interest was apparent by 1763,[11] and the mounting pressure of the crown on mantuano control of municipal and provincial governments progressively heightened that interest.[12] Mantuano interest probably was due in part to the vanity cited by Magnus Mörner as a cause for abundant purchase of military titles,[13] although purchase was prohibited by the *Reglamento para las milicias disciplinadas* which ended the autonomy of proprietary right in a commission. In any case, class and individual self-interest were inextricably blended with whatever degree of vanity was involved.

The militia structure was given a focus by the assignment of a Veteran Battalion of 918 men to Caracas in 1768. It was reinforced in 1771 by the Lombardy Regiment. The veteran force was commanded by the Teniente del Rey, the second ranking official of the Province of Caracas, whose office was created in Venezuela in 1778. Detachments of the Veteran Battalion were stationed at La Guaira and at Puerto Cabello as well as Caracas. On January 5, 1769, all men resident in Caracas were enrolled in a house-to-house census. Culpable avoidance led to an order to complete the registration in a two week period beginning February 23, during which time all men aged fifteen to forty-five were to report to city hall their names, addresses, and occupations. The clergy, judges, lawyers, notaries, city officials, agents of guilds, teachers, farmer's agents, doctors, pharmacists, surgeons, government employees, wholesalers, commercial employees, commissionaires, and students were excused. On the basis of the registration the men of Caracas were organized into militia units. The White Battalion was paraded on April 16, that of the Pardos on April 20, and that of Morenos on May 4.[14] New regulations were issued in 1771 for the militia battalions of whites and pardos in Caracas, in Valles de Aragua, in Valle de Valencia, and for the militia squadron of cavalry of Caracas. The military obligations and exemptions of all free Venezuelans, ages fifteen to forty-five, were restated. Enforcement was improved when the intendancy system was introduced on a provincial basis in 1776 and the Captain-General was made superintendent in 1783. At the time of the Gual and España republican rebellion of 1799 a detachment of the Queen's Regiment was assigned to duty in Caracas.[15]

At the turn of the century there were 13,126 men in the regular army and militia units in Venezuela. About thirteen per cent were regulars and these plus some 3500 militiamen constituted the active duty force. The Puerto Cabello-La Guaira-Caracas triangle, the strategic core of Venezuela, had some 7300 men on active duty or readily mobilized. The eastern provinces, most easily invaded from foreign colonies, had the second most important concentration in the Cumaná area with some 2900 men on duty or easily mobilized. The remaining 2900 were distributed in decreasing order of importance at Maracaibo, Guayana, and Isla Margarita.[16]

Service in the militia was a source of prestige and the highest placed Venezuelans were proud to command militia battalions. Units were segregated according to color: white, mixed bloods, and Negro. Non-white officers serving mixed blood and Negro units could hold no higher rank than that of captain.[17] Militiamen had to attend their unit drill sessions, the annual assembly, fulfill other duties as demanded, and live within a stated distance of the village in which their unit headquarters were located.[18]

II

Militia units existing in 1810 provided the first armed force for the revolutionary regime in Venezuela. The forces, both regular and militia, stationed in the Province of Caracas joined the rebellion from the beginning. Captain General Emparán handed over control of the units in the province by designating a new commandant imposed by the rebels. Emparán called in all unit commanders and other officers and replaced them with agents of the rebels. The new appointees included eighteen Peninsulars of whom only three left the patriot cause.[19] As the ebb and flow of combat, of victory and defeat, of formation and collapse and renewal of governments occurred the militia became almost indistinguishable from other forces, although the names of units and the kind of commission held by an officer indicated some continuity of distinction between army and militia personnel. Reorganization began after the defeat of the major Spanish forces in Venezuela was completed in 1823. Mopping-up operations continued as late as 1829, however, against royalist guerrillas. Reorganization was complicated in 1823 by a squabble over who commanded local civic militia units: the Intendant of the Department or the Commanding General of the Department. The latter won out on the grounds that the true base of security in Venezuela was the militia since the republic could not afford a large permanent army.[20]

The congress of Colombia, which had authorized in the Law of May 6, 1824, a permanent force of 50,000 men, moved to establish the militia, especially after the executive branch issued a decree in August 1824 ordering the enrollment of all men from eighteen to fifty years of age in the militia. General hostility to the levy of 13,000 men for the army ordered May 24, 1824, was especially strong among civilian liberals in Caracas, Valencia, and Turmero, as well as in other parts of Colombia, and led to suspension of recruiting and resort to militia. Organization of the militia on a legal basis was necessary and congress went to work on a militia law.[21] The bill was forwarded to the presidency at the end of session in 1825, where the Council of State proposed a drastic revision on the grounds that the bill called for an unrealistic number of units and far too much money. The Secretary of War proposed instead two categories of militia, the disciplined (later auxiliary) and the civic. Government would finance only the former.[22] The revision was given final form by Santander who proposed two categories of militia based on age and kind of service expected. Auxiliary militiamen, ages eighteen to thirty-five, were to be a reserve army. Local or municipal militiamen, ages fourteen to eighteen and thirty-five to fifty, plus the physically unfit, and all who had completed military service in the army would serve the needs of public order in the locality. The auxiliary militia was to be controlled and trained by the commanding generals of departments, and the local militia by civil authorities.[23]

The Law of April 18, 1826, organized the armed forces and provided for a national militia. The assigned missions of the army, navy, and national militia were the defense of the nation against external and internal dangers and the maintenance of public order.[24] Within ninety days a *Guardia Cívica* unit of seven hundred men had been formed in Caracas. Its organization coincided with the crisis of the Cosiata and its prompt formation undoubtedly reflected the intention to resist repression of rebellion against the government of Colombia. The Guardia Cívica was made up of eight companies and its members bought their own uniforms.[25] In 1829 Páez as Superior Military and Civil Chief of Venezuela regulated the militia. The disciplined militia had been on duty status since October 18, 1827. For many duty status meant being on the alert, more frequent drill, no travel without permission, and enjoyment of fuero, but otherwise the men in the disciplined militia carried on their civilian life. Some units, however, were on regular garrison duty. The 1829 decree reviewed and insisted on these provisions and ordered all men of ages fourteen to fifty not yet enrolled to be so in their parishes. Local officials would command them. The newly enrolled men in each canton were to be divided into inactive auxiliary militia and civic militia units, but nothing was expected of them beyond enrollment for the time being. Inactive auxiliary militia units were made the source of replacements for the army and for auxiliary militia units on active duty. In addition they had to meet any local need in the absence of active auxiliary militia units. The civic militia would serve local needs along with inactive auxiliary militia units.[26]

Developments affecting the militia between 1826 and 1830 were linked to the domination of Venezuela during those years by officers of the armies of independence. They moved into public office at all levels of government, heightening the friction between the armed forces and the civilian side of government developing since 1817.[27] There were commanding generals in the departments, jefes superiores in the districts, commandants of arms in the provinces, military commandants in the cantons and even in the parishes. They were a law unto themselves, and they were protected by military fuero to which the militia was also subject. "The whole people saw itself removed from the authority of ordinary courts. Men without other merit than their diligent travel carrying messages and reports easily received military rank denied to old and meritorious soldiers that had acquired their [grade] at the price of their blood in the battles of independence." Therefore military courts intervened in the whole life of the people.[28]

The decay of whatever professional standards the officers had picked up was rapid, enhanced by political promotional standards already indicated. Thus Páez built his machine to check the ambitions of highly placed rival veteran officers of independence, the Libertadores, seeking power in Venezuela. By bringing the men into the militia under fuero, Páez in part removed them from the authority of the veteran officers holding civil office. The militia provided a frame of political organization, fuero a legal base for Páez's authority over "party" members, the whole made palatable by his prestige.

In 1830 the congress made all men from eighteen to forty years of age members of the active militia which would include infantry, artillery, and cavalry units. In each province the governor was to enroll all the men and form them into units. The actual registration and organization took place at cantonal and parish levels of government. Each parish was expected to furnish a militia company. Officers and noncommissioned officers were elected by members of their units, and congress hoped that capable veteran officers no longer in military service would be chosen. Units were to hold roll call and drill on feast days. Militiamen were required to uniform, arm, and supply themselves. Those who could not, after verification, would be supplied by the government. Units would always serve under their own officers and were subject to two kinds of duty besides drill sessions. The most frequent duty was municipal which was nonmilitary and unpaid.[29]

Tosta García in his *Costumbres caraqueños* narrated a tale with the flavor of such duty. Don Temístocles had been moaning about night patrol duty in Caracas to his three companions. One of them remarked, "You are right, Don Temístocles . . . it has become unsupportable. Every night comes one to the door of your house from the *comisario de la cuadra* who in the voice of a determined mother-in-law says: 'Tonight you have the second quarter of patrol. If you do not come, three days in jail and a 10 pesos fine.' " But another protested, "Don't you know . . . that it is the duty of the associated to protect each other?" [30]

For municipal duty the militia units were divided into groups of twelve and each group was liable for duty during the assigned month. Municipal duties included escorting prisoners, conducting gold shipments, guarding jails, pursuing criminals, and the like. Military duty was a rarer obligation. The active militia could be ordered to military duty by any one of the several levels of civil authority. An active militia unit could be required to serve anywhere in the nation on military duty, but usually served in its own or adjoining provinces. Duty outside the home province was limited to a month and within it to two months. These periods could be extended for grave need. In addition to the active militia there was a local militia of all men of ages forty to sixty years. The local militia served only in its own canton and was expected to be self-equipped. It was called on only when the active militia units were out on military service.[31] Men whose professions or public offices were in obvious conflict with militia service were excused. Immediate resistance to both types of militia units was noted, supporting the thesis of the Villa of Aragua that fuero was the main reason for joining the militia which provided raw material to organize armies. The Congress of 1830 ordered vigorous enforcement of the law to organize militia and to exact of it the services assigned.[32]

The militia was reorganized on a more practical basis in 1836, but local control over the militia was reconfirmed. The age limit was reduced to forty-five years. Although the two categories of militia were retained, assignment to one or the other category was simply based on economics. If a Venezuelan could afford to buy his uniform, provide a gun and bayonet, and supply the basic number of forty cartridges, he was assigned to the active militia. In addition he had to be resident in the cantonal seat of government or in another town designated by the president as an active militia locale. If a Venezuelan did not meet these economic and residential requirements, he was in the reserve (local) militia. Officers of the active militia were named by the president from lists supplied by the governors of provinces, but they continued to be elected in the reserve militia from lists supplied by the government.[33]

A first step in coordinating military service of the active militia and activity of the permanent army was provided in 1841 through the Commandants of Arms (*comandantes de armas*). In redressing the civil-military relationship in 1830, congress had abolished the "military commandants, both principal and subaltern, that had been created contrary to the law by the preceding administration in almost all the towns, cantons, and circuits," as well as the Commanding Generals of the Departments. Congress created in turn the

Commandants of Arms in seven coastal provinces and on Isla Margarita for defense against invasion. These commands consisted of an officer, a second in command, and one or two adjutants plus any military force assigned to his defense region. Congress carefully stated that a commandant's authority was not tied to a specific territorial jurisdiction, but was limited only to the personnel assigned him. For all else he must rely on local civil authorities.[34] Apparently experience in the sedition of 1831, the War of the Reforms of 1835, the rebellion of the Farfanes in 1837 and of other lesser guerrillas led congress to augment the authority of the commandants of arms to include command over the active militia when ordered to military duty by the governor within the commandant's defense zone. The commandants of arms were deprived, however, of their fixed term of office which had given them a temporary proprietary right in their duties.[35]

Laws organizing the militia also provided for a militia staff of veterans in eight key provinces and one or more drill instructors for each province. In practice, however, only a few provinces had a militia organization in being, and the national government did not appoint a full complement of commandants of arms, veteran staffs, nor drill instructors. In 1842–1843 the national budget provided for six veteran staffs and thirteen instructors, but in practice there were veteran staffs in two provinces, no instructors, and five commandants of arms.[36] Where militia units existed they were usually found in the most densely populated sector of the province, normally the capital city area. Governors were interested in the militia as a device to maintain public order and to bring the people out of the bush into town on Sundays, making them personally aware of the local and national community to which they belonged but from which they so commonly lived and died apart.[37] Conflicting laws, however, gave both governors and commandants of arms the right to direct troop movements, and no amount of effort by the executive branch sufficed to persuade the congress to end the overlapping authority of the two officials.[38] Finally, establishment of a federal government deprived the national authority of the right to appoint commandants of arms.[39]

III

The primary reliance of government on the militia, manifested in 1831 and 1835, continued in the 1840's. Of the rebellion of 1846–1847, General Páez observed that the volunteer army had "organized itself prodigiously" in a few days out of veterans of the war for independence and civilian property owners and workers.[40] His report was confirmed by veteran Brigadier General Pedro Hernández of the Armies of the Republic who served as chief of cavalry units for the parishes of Santa María de Ipire, Altamira, Iguana, Espino, Santa Rita, and Cabruta of the Canton of Chaguaramas. Hernández praised his militia force whose members had mounted, armed, and maintained themselves.[41] The dispersed regular forces were not a factor in the defeat of the uprising. The permanent army's assigned function was national defense and only secondarily that of domestic order, which was the primary concern of the militia. The active or national militia whose function was the maintenance of public order was not ready for service, except for a few units, although it was the "principal force with which the nation counts for providing its security." [42] A report on a militia force operating against the faction noted that the six militia companies had 223 guns distributed as follows: two companies had none, the other four had from 34 to 73 muskets, and the advance party had 40 firearms.[43]

The ruling groups, heartened by the success of the militia in the 1846–1847 rebellion, counted heavily on it to guarantee their continued dominance of government. Newly elected President Monágas, however, broke with Páez and his Conservative allies, surrounded himself with the men whom Páez had defeated in past rebellions, and seriously undertook the organization of the reserve militia of "proletarians who lack the means to pay for their armaments and uniform."[44] Monágas would make the reserve militia, whose existence was his work and whose officers were his appointees, his chief reliance. He disarmed the active militia which represented the propertied element and which controlled the choice of its officers. Monágas erected his network of alliances with lesser caudillos through the reserve militia which became his means for controlling provincial government.[45]

As its last resort, the "oligarchy's" congressional majority planned to impeach Monágas, seize control of government, order the active militia to duty under martial law, put Páez in command, and make him responsible to congress instead of to the presidency.[46] Monágas proved more popular than the congress, however, and that body was cowed by the assassination of some of its members by reserve militia units of Caracas who have been labelled the "lowest of the people."[47] The brief subsequent rebellion headed by Páez gave the government cause to call to active duty a large number of men. By 1849 the administration claimed units in 10 provinces with 37,500 infantry, 3,800 cavalry, and 200 artillery militiamen.[48] Monágas sent the army and the reserve militia into the field for fighting and charged the active militia with preservation of local order. In justification the administration alleged that the active militia was hard to organize and only the reserve militia had been of value.[49]

The second Monagan president, José Gregorio, secured the reorganization of the militia in 1854. He did not touch the right of local officials of province, canton, or parish to order the militia to duty for public order purposes.[50] The militia law of 1854 kept only one category of militia. All men of eighteen to fifty years had to serve. Units could be ordered to duty for the duration of an emergency for service anywhere in the nation. Officers were designated by the national government and all personnel were subject to military regulations when on active duty and paid by the nation. Any Venezuelan who did not meet his militia obligation was sentenced to the permanent army. Militiamen continued to be on a roster for municipal service, but a forty-eight hour limit for such duty was set.[51] The government was still trying in 1856 to organize the militia effectively and claimed at least skeleton success in 1857.[52] After 1880 the militia was known simply as the reserve and units called to peacetime duty were known as supernumerary units of the army.[53] A move to relinquish the use of supernumerary units made in 1897 had to be abandoned because of the revolutions of 1898 and 1902–1903.[54]

The military code of 1882 established the militia as the source from which the states drafted their manpower quotas for the army, and the provision was continued in the military code of 1904.[55] According to Arcaya the basic social division after 1882 became that of the recruitable and the non-recruitable men of society.[56] The president in 1891 asked congress for a militia law obliging every citizen to serve when called,[57] but the inequitable enforcement of service obligations continued.[58] The militia continued to be as indifferently developed, despite the laws, as during the Páez and Monagan eras. Municipal service performed as part of militia duty remained unpopular. The persistent effort to make the militia a kind of government party to mobilize an effective majority of opinion in support of the personalities in public office did not rally the people to militia enlistment. The decentralization of control under the federal reorganization of Venezuela did not advance the cause of an effective militia.

President Antonio Guzmán Blanco, who initiated the era of despotic caudillism, was ill-pleased with the ineffectiveness of the militia as a means of preserving public order and the stability of government. The militia was slow to enter a campaign because of the difficulties of assembling the necessary supplies and war matériel, thus enabling an ambitious caudillo to build a following on the basis of his early victories.[59] Guzmán Blanco divided the country into five districts in 1879 headed by men known as military or national delegates whose particular function was the prompt assembly and equipping of militia units in the face of revolt.[60] The device of the national delegate was probably based on President Linares Alcántara's use of personal agents called delegates to calm the turbulence among state and local caudillos who were weary of the repressive measures of Guzmán Blanco's seven-year administration. The chief effect of the new system which remained the standard solution for the problem was to give form and legal basis to the role of the regional caudillos who influenced or controlled the appointments of state presidents and other officials. They also served as a channel of communication between the president of the nation and state officials, and through the militia as a more direct means for the president to contact some of the people.

A military delegate appointed during a quiet time would have to build his political following. Thus in mid-1898, General José Ignacio Pulido arrived at Coro, capital of the State of Falcón, as the new chief of the 2nd Military Region. In his attempt to affirm his political authority he moved directly into the parish level of politics and did not work out an alliance with General Gregorio Segura Riera, President of Falcón. General Riera proved to have more influence with the President of Venezuela. General Pulido was removed.[61]

As a new level of authority, the national delegates were soon regarded as a disaster. General Briceño Ayestarán has written most eloquently of the national delegates sent to the State of Los Andes. They named provincial governors who were changed as frequently as were the delegates. A delegate brought with him a retinue of clients for offices in the states under his jurisdiction: governors, state cabinet members, jefes civiles for districts, administrators of public revenues, secretaries, jefes de policía, and the rest of the offices. In addition he had his *mesnada*, a numerous body-guard, which he supported through forced loans from the wealthy and the business community. The Táchira, Briceño Ayestarán's favorite region of the State of Los Andes, was also visited by commandants of arms who apparently had become to the provinces in the states what the national delegates were to the regions and the states. Commandants of arms also had their mesnadas maintained in the usual way, but they travelled more. They seized supplies, pack mules, and mounts from stores and individuals, a practice which sometimes served as a device for obtaining cash through the return of property for a fee.[62] Guzmán Blanco did nothing to correct the situation, possibly because he had maintained his own mesnada, an 800-man bodyguard whom he rewarded as he was leaving office in 1877 with a distribution of 69,000 pesos and other gifts, including lands in the vicinity of the capital city.[63] During the administrations of Rojas Paúl and of Andueza Palacios no delegates were sent to the Andes. The evil then resumed there in worse form than ever.[64]

Abusive practices of the delegates and their retinues forced the Tachirenses to take control of Los Andes and then to move more vigorously into national politics to protect their interests. The men of the mountains, the Andinos, descended to the plains to impose order on Venezuela. They were largely alien to the family groupings of central and eastern Venezuela and possessed no links with the local and regional oligarchies outside the mountains. The Andinos displaced and dominated those elements that had so long controlled national political life and had plundered the relative abundance of the Andean area.[65]

As the main source of manpower for the army, the militia, "organized" and controlled by the states, was affected by the mounting interest in an effective army. Under federal organization the Minister of the Interior was the main channel for relations between the states and the national government. The ministry attempted to get state cooperation in developing an improved army. The states apparently ignored an 1893 request that they comply fully with the militia laws which had been largely unenforced for some years. In 1895 the states were ordered to comply and to report their achievements within six weeks.[66] The government expected a militia force of 200,000 men. Instead President Crespo complained to congress that the states were not meeting their obligation to supply contingents for the armed forces.[67] No evidence of general compliance has been found. The system of national delegates, in itself a militia reform, continued to be a recourse of the national government, but the delegates relied much more on their personal political machines, their mesnadas, and the levies their local caudillos and caciques could bring into being. In any case in the main periods of anarchic conflict the militia, technically embodying every Venezuelan man, dissolved into a multitude of fighting groups and reassembled into larger units through the caudillesque alliances which divided Venezuelans into two rival forces struggling to occupy the posts of leadership in Venezuelan society.

The era of the militia formally closed with the Law for the Formation and Renewal of the Forces of Land and Sea of June 24, 1919. Its role as the reserve force and as the source of replacements for the regular units was terminated. Conscription supplied the men previously requisitioned from the militia units under state control. Once a conscript's tour of duty was over he entered the reserve. The militia was not directly attacked or mentioned in the law. Its continuation simply was not provided for.[68]

7 | THE MILITARY

The history of the Venezuelan army has been one of long-delayed achievement of professionalism. Venezuela possessed a disciplined militia organization in the colonial period, some units of which saw extended duty. Venezuela experienced something approaching the nation in arms during the war for independence, and then reverted to a primary reliance on the militia. "Many years would be needed so that the career of arms would not continue being a necessity of the moment, a transitory activity imposed by the circumstance of internal revolts, subject to the contingencies of politics and personal ambitions of a sequence of caudillos, but a firm and certain military profession, based on modern scientific teachings of the art of war." [1] Another officer stated in a 1938 radio broadcast that until the end of the nineteenth century "the army as a national institution ceased to be." [2] When professionalization began in Venezuela it reflected that of the modern major powers, but it began much later than in some other Latin American countries. Thus Magnus Mörner has designated the mid-nineteenth century as a terminal point for the era in Latin America in which many military chiefs were self-commissioned leaders of gangs or prominent civilians accorded a military title as a recognition of their importance. The last half of the century saw the establishment of the military academy and the formation of the professionally-trained career officer. Socially the change was marked by a growing disengagement between the officer corps and other social groups.[3]

The distinction between military and militia units was clearly maintained in the provincial constitutions drafted before the Spanish reconquest of most of Venezuela in 1812. Abolition of fuero was ordered in the charter of the Province of Barcelona and it was limited in that of the Province of Caracas which excluded military men but not militiamen from public office.[4] The Federal Constitution of 1811 limited fuero to those men actually in service, declared the militia the "most convenient and secure national defense for a free state," and limited the number of professional soldiers to the irreducible minimum compatible with national security as authorized by congress. The military power was to be kept in due subordination to civil authority.[5]

The provinces set up both permanent armies and militia organizations. The Province of Caracas apparently intended to maintain a small corps of military officers, a regular force of three battalions, and a fully organized militia force. It sought to avoid the tyranny implicit in the use of an armed

minority to dominate the rest of the people. The provincial
government intended to reform the old system in which
some militia units were ordered to permanent duty so that
the "farmers and artisans of a single town or jurisdiction,
[were] separated almost 20 years from fields and shops, torn
from their families, submerged in the misery of long inter-
ruption of their work, cast into destructive climates where
they have perished, and finally, degraded and corrupted
with the inactivity in detachments and garrisons. Veteran
units, always incomplete, ill-disciplined, were composed up
to six years ago of European recruits, generally criminals
taken from the prisons whom the change of climate and
their vices destroyed, leaving decimated skeleton units, and
consequently burdening the Militia with an undue work
that has delayed the progress of the population and general
prosperity." [6] The assertion about veteran units was confirmed by the Royal Decree of July 28, 1766, which provided that vagos who deserted from assigned military duty
should serve eight years in the regiments stationed in
America.[7]

The revolutionary regime planned to give officers the
essential core of specialized military knowledge at an Academy of Mathematics and other subjects in garrison training. Garrisons were to run primary schools to educate corporals as the basic noncommissioned officer grade. The
Mathematics Academy was scheduled to open September 3,
1810, to train military men from the ages of twelve to thirty-
two as well as any other youth with scientific aptitude.[8]
To sweeten the system and in recognition "that reward
and punishment are the two bases of the military structure . . . ," promotions were announced in the *Gaceta de
Caracas* of May 18, 1810, for officers of the Company of

Grenadiers of the Veteran Battalion of Caracas, the White Militia Battalion of Caracas, and the Disciplined Militia Cavalry Squadron. In addition the pardo units were restored in Caracas, Aragua, and Valencia, and two new militia cavalry units were authorized for Valencia and the Valles de Aragua.[9] The military strength of Caracas compared to that of other provinces in the Venezuelan federation was a source of anxiety to the *Sociedad Patriótica*, the most influential organization in revolutionary politics at the time. Moreover, the society pointed out to the Supreme Government in October 1811 that the command of the armed forces had become a family operation of the Ayalas.[10]

To counteract subversive royalist efforts, the authorities published July 13, 1811, a detailed mobilization plan for the citizens of Caracas and its outlying areas. It provided for collection of weapons, rationing of supplies, and establishment of street patrols to keep order. Five days later a proclamation (*bando*) ordered all men fifteen to fifty years of age to enlist for possible duty by registering with municipal authorities in Caracas. Enrollees were to bring whatever arms they had and would be trained in their use.[11] The next measure, unsuccessful in its intent to prevent the collapse of the first republic of Venezuela, was a declaration of martial law on June 19, 1812. The regulations incorporated in the decree imposing military government were a precedent for subsequent patriot practice. The generalissimo was authorized to name military chiefs or commanders of villages, towns, cities, and districts. The commissioned officials possessed "primary authority" and civil officials were told to cooperate in every way on matters touching security and defense, as well as to limit their activities strictly to administration of justice and of policía.

The powers of the military officers included recruiting, arming, and organizing troops for duty with the army and also their provisioning, civil defense, morale, and punishment of traitors and suspects. They were empowered to name their own *asesores* and to decree anything necessary to fulfill their assigned functions. The sacrifice of civilian interests included suspension of salaries for civil officials, prohibitions of intellectual pursuits to able-bodied young males, and a levy on all non-ordained religious personnel.[12] The general collapse of independent government, although it was briefly restored in 1813–1814, brought to an end efforts to establish regular army units, until Bolívar returned to organize a fighting force, consolidating the irregular units still fighting Spanish forces into the army of the republic.

The wars for independence were fought by citizen forces whose leaders were practical experts formed by militia training and by guerrilla experience. The army of the period has been described as a composite of armed contingents obeying natural leaders who had subordinated themselves to the public power.[13] These heterogeneous groups of all sizes were carefully pulled together and integrated into a manageable force of some discipline in 1817. Bolívar established his Honor Guard for training and instruction of officers and cadres.[14] In the guerrilla forces the caudillos' personalism was partially tamed by introducing the Napoleonic staff system at army and division level. The staffs were organized in accord with Thiebault's *Manual de Ayudantes Generales de Estado Mayor*, and from them Bolívar drew his experts. The content of formal instruction of troops was provided by manuals and other materials distributed to subordinate officers.[15]

The circumstances attending the consolidation of the

army in 1817 have been described by the acting president of Colombia, Vice President Santander:

> . . . we were forced to make war like the Tartars. What times! Frequently I blushed to see thwarted the ideas I indicated with order, method, and system. . . . There were times when it was necessary to convert the system into disorder and to entice recruits with booty and looting. What discipline could you expect to have in troops composed of such men? There was only one law which obligated us: to fight the *godos,* and to obey it we could not worry about the means. Thus there were troops, that is to say men armed against Spaniards, and they were the founders of the Republic in which we presently live. To uproot suddenly ideas so horrible and to check the excesses of those that have been enlisted by them under the flag of liberty was and is a work very superior to our strength and to our actual condition. To know better what our military system has been, it is necessary that you should have seen that which was called an army three years ago, and from that point would come the conviction that we have advanced much in a very short time. I do not want to say by this that we can stop working to perfect the military system; no sir; we must see to it that our armies merit the name, and that they are terrible only to the enemies of independence. The best means to prevent disorders is to keep the soldier well paid, well dressed, and well assisted; thus he has less need of excess, the chief has more reason and right to punish him.[16]

Unhappily, the Republic of Colombia could not do that and meet the campaign expenses in Ecuador, Peru, and Bolivia. In the spring of 1823 the treasury was empty and "in Venezuela the army would have been absolutely dissolved if by chance we had not been able to use 150,000 pesos deposited in cajas proceeding from Europe." [17]

The capture of Puerto Cabello, Spain's last foothold in northern South America, at the end of 1823 should have meant some relief from the burdens of war for the citizens of Colombia, but major campaigning continued in Peru and Bolivia through December 1824. Still Spain would not admit defeat and imposed on the weary people and the financially desperate government of Colombia a continuing burden of preparedness. Even so, a compromise between an assessment of security needs and the actual capability of Colombia had to be made. It was necessary to conciliate tumultuous resistance to further army recruiting in 1825 and to respond to the penury of the treasury. Government hoped to develop a serviceable national militia while it reduced the regular force by retirement and reduction to inactive status of much of the officer corps. It proposed also to reduce the permanent force stationed in Colombia to four full-strength battalions instead of the larger number of partially manned units in existence. In addition the military court system was organized, the right to fuero was regulated, the staffs of army, division, and departments were reorganized, and the practice of assigning recruits to duty away from their home departments was introduced.[18]

Acting President of Colombia Santander reviewed the use of such terms as *milicias* (militia) and *milicia* (the art of war or the military profession). He also made it clear that if a person had once become an officer in the armed forces the government seldom allowed him to dissociate himself completely from that experience. Such a person was recallable in case of need. Only individuals absolutely discharged—the implication appears to be that they were normally enlisted personnel—were completely freed of military control. On the whole, the practice does not seem very different from present United States practice. The one important difference was the enjoyment of fuero as long as the retired or inactive officer had some formal connection with a staff or some unit with obligation to appear at least once a year at a general review which also entitled him to his retirement or inactive status pay.[19]

The war for independence developed two main categories of higher ranking officers. The larger category was that drawn from one-time guerrilla leaders, from militia officers out of the colonial era, and from those officers developed within the wartime army for whom a professional career held no direct interest. From this number came the first generation of republican caudillos for the most part. The second category, considerably smaller in number, was made up of the quasi-professional and profession-oriented officers. They were led by an elite, close-knit Venezuelan group referred to as the Bolivarians. They possessed a community of purpose and response based on common staff training and experience in warfare and administration outside of Venezuela. As long as Bolívar lived he was the focus towards which all their activities were directed. In the disintegrating Republic of Colombia after 1825 they tried to supply Bolívar's deficiencies as a politician, a role which he refused to play. After Bolívar's death they continued to be a loosely knit team with no star or dominant figure. They failed to keep the Republic of Colombia together because of the force of nationalism and of the more effective leadership by caudillos. They would also fail to seize and shape the destiny of their homeland. The failure was probably due to separation of military and political commands imposed by law.[20]

As long as the conflict with Spain continued, the crises of security supplied justification for maintaining a military structure paralleling the ordinary political offices with preëminence over the civilian structure. Veterans not on active status moved into political offices. The reknitting of military and political functions began with the designation of Páez as Superior Military and Civil Chief of Venezuela in 1827 and was followed in 1828 and 1829 by the extension of that office to the lower Magdalena, the interior of Nueva Granada, and to Ecuador. The four Superior Military and Civil Chiefs were directly subordinated to Bolívar, but those of Venezuela and of Ecuador enjoyed a degree of autonomy which facilitated their prompt separation. In Venezuela, moreover, the office passed into the hands of a caudillo, José Antonio Páez. The remaining three were headed by Bolivarians.

Few of the Venezuelan officers who distinguished themselves in service with Bolívar in campaigns outside their native land made a successful transfer to political leadership. Bolívar had kept with him as he left Venezuela to push into Nueva Granada and on southward to Ecuador, Peru, and Bolivia the officers of talent developing a professional attitude. Men like José Antonio Páez and José Tadeo Monágas were left in Venezuela for sound military and political reasons, but as much because their strength lay in their incarnation of the non-patrician Venezuelan milieu. Páez, like Antaeus, with his feet deep-rooted in the rubble of revolution and the yeasty mass of social ferment would be more than a match for the Bolivarians who needed an adequate professional army to accomplish their purpose. The Bolivarians were a century and more ahead of their time. The caudillos were men of their time.

Professionalization of the natural leaders did not go much beyond improving their technique as leaders. Once the fighting was over these natural leaders were forced to find other fields for their talent. Their alternatives were, for a few, corporate oblivion in garrison life on starvation pay; for the many, the loneliness of economic struggle on farm and ranch or in shop, craft, trade, or profession; and also for the many a search for political preëminence in the new national community in a manner consonant with the forms of tradition: posts in government with enjoyment of fuero. The nationalism and the will to rule among the Venezuelan officers produced by the war of independence also made the choice a natural one. In the mid-1820's José Antonio Páez epitomized the point of view of the Venezuelan veterans that the free nation of Colombia was their creation and at least in the Venezuelan sector its leadership was their right and obligation. Failure to exercise that right would enable the onlookers to the struggle to take over and consume the fruit of their effort.[21]

A quarter century after the fall of Puerto Cabello the capable leadership trained in the war for independence was largely incapacitated. New guerrilla leaders replaced the veterans as they sought to emulate the veteran officer's quest for social command. There were no military academies to train professionals, no major international wars to "educate by doing," no military ladder of success in serving the national community. After 1830 the permanent armed forces were in fact no more than minor reserve security units for internal service, enjoying some fuero and still subject for half a century to the old colonial disciplinary regulations of the militia. The armed forces did not prosper under caudillism. Successful national caudillos were wholly self-centered. They maintained no officer schools, no reserves under army control, and virtually destroyed the prestige of military service.[22] Technical needs of the artillery were supposed to be met by the Academy of Mathematics attached to the university in Caracas, but it trained mostly engineers and surveyors.[23] There were naval schools, but their graduates were mainly merchant mariners and pilots.[24] During the nineteenth century only the naval officers may be considered to have possessed the rudiments of a professional schooling. It is no exaggeration to state that the caudillos of Venezuela, whether veterans of the war for independence or emergent from subsequent civil conflict, were not the product of an institution or of a rationale, but of an appetite.

The nation in arms had failed to develop a professional army as it emerged from its struggle for independence. It did possess a general anti-military attitude. The reasons were grave and numerous. Civilian hostility had been aroused by the inexorable exactions of men and property in the war effort. The amoral, lawless, and capricious conduct of many men of all grades and ranks in the armed forces undermined the prestige of the Libertadores.[25] The acting president was conscious of it as he noted that "they are my enemies only because I wear a soldier's uniform, and I do not have five shelves of books." [26]

A low standard of living for men in the ranks did not improve the repute of military service. The standard contrasted oddly with the heavy post-campaigning needs which in 1826 accounted for nearly eighty percent of a fifteen million peso budget. Even so, many officers were on inactive status with half or one-third pay. Only 228 officers with the rank of lieutenant colonel or above were in active service and 28 of these were in nonmilitary posts.[27] Set off against this situation was the fact that national government income for Colombia was estimated at six million pesos for 1826.

Inevitably obligations could not be met. By mid-year the commanding generals of the departments of the republic were inundating the Ministry of War with reports of inability to maintain and feed the troops, who in turn took it out on the civilian population. The recognized solution was dismissal of much of the army, but Spain still refused to acknowledge defeat. In 1827 the government decided to dismiss half the 12,000 troops stationed in the northern provinces, but military economy measures were wiped out during Bolívar's dictatorship.[28]

In Venezuela the ambition of Páez and the anti-military orientation of his allies in the patriciate had a corrosive effect on professional military values and career opportunities. It was made continuous by nearly constant civil conflict during the era of the caudillos. Defeat of government forces in civil conflict was commonly followed by dismissal, imprisonment, or exile of their chiefs, most of the officers, and many of the noncommissioned officers. Even an elected president could deem it wise to make such a sweeping change.[29] Dismissal under these conditions could cost a would-be career officer his chance for promotion and the loss of pension and other retirement benefits. The gravest evil, eventually carried to ridiculous extremes, was the inflation in military grades. Despite the inflated numbers of men with commissions, and the fact that the inflation was most obvious in the higher ranks, the sources consulted for this study leave the impression that a career officer seldom obtained the rank of general. On the whole it seems only slightly temerarious to affirm that the title of general lost most of its military meaning and acquired almost wholly a political value.

II

In Latin America the main occasions for the development of militarism roughly correspond to those in other parts of the world. The peril, from the non-military point of view, arises after victory or defeat in international conflict and during domestic turbulence. After international conflict the army has emerged as the most powerful pressure group in society and army leaders have demanded due recognition of their importance. After victory they seek their reward and after defeat they would remake the nation, strengthening it and eliminating the allegedly venal incompetent leadership which has made defeat possible. In Latin America, however, the more usual opportunity for militarism has been the transitional period of socio-political change involved in the liquidation of a dictatorship or the effort of established ruling groups to prevent a social threat.[30] Exploitation of such opportunities demands that the armed forces be materially the strongest institution or pressure group. In the Venezuelan situation after the long war for independence the Libertadores held political control with official government sanction. For example, in making appointments to the six free intendancies and the seventeen free provinces of Colombia in 1823, twenty-one of the twenty-three appointees were higher ranking officers.[31] The inherent division in the Libertadores between the Bolivarians and the veterans, between corporate professionalism and anarchic individual ambition, prevented the development of a long-term dominant role for the armed forces. The denial of political control to the professional military was assisted by the inability of the nation to support a military force adequate to such an end and by a regrouping of the property owners and intellectuals around a caudillo.

As the moment for Venezuelan secession from Colombia approached, the rapacious anarchic greed of the Libertadores was reaching its peak in the monopolization of public office. The effort made in the law of 1826 reorganizing the army to limit commissioned personnel on active duty status was overridden by congress itself in 1827 after Bolívar took up his duties as president.[32] Colombian Minister of Interior José Manuel Restrepo confided to his diary in October 1829:

Everything has come to be military. The Liberator and the Minister of War have handed out an infinity of grades and promotions and all the world is general or colonel. The revolutions in Colombia are the work of the military. The towns would never be in turmoil if [the officers] were not seducing and leading them as is clear from the history of disturbances since 1826.

From such military as these has come the evil that in Colombia civil authorities are nothing; the military do not respect them and when an order does not please them, they do not obey it. To this evil the military fuero, granted to the militia, has contributed; since the militia are spread throughout the republic, there is hardly a parish in which they do not exist; moreover, all the useful men are controlled by the military and they make a joke of civil authorities; thus it is that by this and other measures almost all the government has become military.[33]

Even Páez was reputed to have taken part in the political and economic profiteering made possible by the disorder in society. He was alleged to have treated his llaneros badly, buying up their land script at two to five per cent of face value. He was also charged with exercising a monopoly over the sale of meat, of gambling, and auctioning of tithe collections in the 1820's. Thus his role in the Cosiata or Valencia Insurrection of 1826 may be made to appear as a mere expression of financial self-interest.[34] To offset that report was Páez's offer to sell his properties in Apure at a reasonable price to the government for bonds at five per cent interest in order to continue land and cattle distribution to veterans there endangered by lack of government funds.[35] In any case Páez and the militia which became the device for effective organized action by the property-owning element would abruptly check the disorder in Venezuela.

The Constituent Congress of 1830 faced up to the mounting problem of political excesses and ambitions of the Libertadores by limiting military fuero and by insisting on civilian control of government and military functions including command in the militia. The latter provision contravened both colonial and Colombian practice.[36] In addition the militia was detached from direct army control, and the army never again in the nineteenth century regained exclusive authority over it. Moreover, congress prevented further growth of the officer corps in the 1830's by restating the principle that promotions and appointments in permanent army units would be held to the table of organization. Congress limited the army to three battalions.[37] Sir Robert Ker-Porter whose long tour of duty in Venezuela began in 1828 as consul, in 1833 labelled the new regime a "nonmilitary system." [38]

After 1830 the Venezuelan government relied on the militia to keep internal order. Because of the unsettled conditions associated with secession from Colombia and an ineffective rebellion in 1831 in favor of federation, restoration of Colombia, and fueros, the new nation began its existence with a force of 5,000 men, mostly militia. The army had a limited number of permanent personnel. The force was dispersed with a thousand men in Táchira on the Granadian frontier and the rest in garrisons in Maracaibo, Valencia, and Puerto Cabello. Congress had authorized calling up more militia for any additional forces deemed necessary. It is apparent that the veteran army of independence was virtually nonexistent. Most of the combat trained officers were on the inactive list and the militia upon which the government was supposed to depend was largely on paper.[39] In good part the action of congress towards the military followed proposals made by José Rafael Revenga to Bolívar in 1829. Yet in 1833 President Páez proposed that the permanent army be reduced from three battalions to two.[40] At the same time Páez invited home a goodly number of high and middle rank officers who were in exile as Bolivarians and as partisans of Gran Colombia. They were restored to the military list.[41] The anti-military sentiment of the patriciate was evident in congressional completion of the vice presidential elections in 1833. None of the twelve candidates had won enough votes. Of the five leading candidates, three were officers of the war of independence. General Soublette with 52 out of a possible 179 electoral votes had twice as many as any other two candidates. Congress elected Navarte who had no commission and who had received 31 electoral votes.[42] To its anti-military posture the patriciate added a discreet anti-caudillism, expressed by its choice of Dr. José María Vargas as president of Venezuela in 1835. The election was the patriciate's bid for dominance, an assertion of supremacy over the influence of Páez.

The army's authorized strength from 1830 to 1835 was about 2500 men divided into 3 infantry battalions of 600 men each, a company of supernumerary infantry, 6 companies of artillery, and a company of cavalry.[43] The Vene-

zuelan government continued to regard the army as a punitive, social reform, and social welfare institution as well as
a means by which the citizen could meet his obligation to
defend his country against foreign attack. A law of May 23,
1836, on the trial and penalties for robbery provided in
Article 43 that the thirteen categories of vagos should be
obliged to serve in the army as a preventive measure. A
vago by definition was considered apt to fall into major
crime and was a social parasite at best.[44]

The situation of the army had not improved at the time
that the War of the Reforms began in 1835. The plotting of
discontented inactive status officers, the Bolivarians, stimulated the junior officers of the veteran Anzoátegui Battalion
to unsuccessful rebellion against the newly installed Vargas
Administration.[45] They "stood alone in the act, unsanc-
tioned by any class of their fellow citizens." [46] The Bolivarians counted on rather widespread discontent to develop
into active support while they held the capital city. The
Caracas coup d'état provided the occasion for the leading
caudillo of the eastern provinces, José Tadeo Monágas, to
lead a rebellion. His program restated the main themes
used to justify resistance to government since 1830: the
need to restore the Republic of Colombia on a federal
basis; an end to persecution of Bolivarians and Libertadores, mainly through restoration of fuero to the army and
the clergy; the recognition of Catholicism as the religion of
the Republic; and full veteran's preference in all government offices.[47]

A British report on the causes of the War of the Reforms
cited the "disease of military ambition," the usual aftermath
of revolution restrainable only by "military despotism."
Bolívar's death had ended that necessary despotism, and

in Venezuela he had been "succeeded by Gen¹ Páez who . . . showed a wish to advance civilians in public estimation, to be a leading feature of his government and manifested every desire to give to it the character of a civil government rather than . . . a military command." The military were bitter but Páez "saw not only what the country wanted from its backwardness in the arts of peace, but also what it did not want in the preponderating influence of a number of turbulent chiefs, who bred in the wave of a revolution, could breathe no air but that of intrigue." Páez could dominate the situation, but "matters assumed another tone to which the election of the president chosen (Dr. Vargas) gave a plausibility—almost an excuse. The military men, who were candidates for the presidency, advanced and those who supported their pretensions (being alike military) insisted upon those claims which personal service and exposure, risk of life, sacrifice of fortune, etc., undoubtedly give. . . ." Their goal was "federalizing the country: that is, splitting it into as many provinces as there are generals who want to be governors." ⁴⁸ To United States Chargé Williamson the possibility remained because the role of Páez as the guarantor of constitutional civil government carried with it the implicit danger, in event of his death, of a revival of the defeated Bolivarian element, of the organization of provincial parties headed by military men.⁴⁹

Official United States reporting on the coup d'état in Caracas brought out other aspects. The military, Bolivarian, and quasi-family character of the movement was asserted. General Pedro Briceño Méndez told the Chargé that the seizure of government was entirely military. The Caracan rebels counted on the discontent in other parts of Venezuela to develop into active support and acceptance of their leadership. Discontent reflected the denial of political office to veteran officers, election frauds, and a demand for reforms. The rebels were joined by the Valencia garrison under leadership of local retired military officers, and in the east General José Tadeo Monágas activated his followers. Rebellion in Maracaibo had already preceded that of Caracas. Success or failure, however, depended on the position taken by Páez, and he again disappointed the Bolivarians by refusing to play their game. He would not take part in a movement to undo what he and the patriciate had accomplished. He would have no part of a movement that was "solely military headed by the family and connections of the late General Bolívar." [50]

Chargé Williamson presented an analysis of the revolutionary process as it had developed in Venezuela:

There is so little general fixed purpose among the revolutionists in this country, that I should perhaps be wrong in saying these movements have any other object than personal ambition or aggrandizement. . . . They set out without an object, but what their own feelings may dictate regardless of public weal or public woe, and it becomes a matter so easy for a designing officer with a few dollars to convert to his own purposes the troops under his command that it is a matter of speculation to raise up a party to advance his pretensions, as the various changes that have been made here, have always ended in reconciliation and a retention in service, and to the command rank he has assumed or was advanced to by a superior officer.

. . . The Gov^t has become sensible that it is necessary to exert its full powers against insurrectionary movements, otherwise it must become a prey even to the few designing ambitious military men whom the revolution has left upon half pay and who cannot exist unless in war or revolution.[51]

Unsuccessful revolt had brought punishment to a few individuals, some 222 pained exiles. Worse was the fate of that still amorphous institution, the army, which as an institution had not been involved. Its further diminution ensued; the government was strengthened in its reliance on the militia which in turn knew little effective development, since "security was vested in public opinion." [52] Officers were not deprived of inactive duty pay and retirement benefits, unless guilty of rebellion, but they were denied the preëminence they had considered their due and were largely removed from any significant public office.[53] Not only was the army reduced, but also a number of fortifications were ordered demolished in 1836 because they were costly to maintain; they had been foci of conspiracy, and they had served as defense points for rebels against government forces.[54] The authorized strength of the permanent armed forces for 1836–1837 fell from 2500 to 1000 men. Officers of the permanent army were to be chosen from those who had demonstrated their loyalty during the War of the Reforms.[55] The latter provision was retained until 1839. In 1838 the actual strength of the army was 800 men,[56] and would fall even lower although the authorized size would remain at 1000 until 1845. Strength was increased to 2,000 for 1846, 1847, and 1848, and was then reduced to 800 men in 1849.[57]

French consular agents in Venezuela reported the diminution of the army. In December 1838 they noted that the military regimen was nonexistent as far as troops were concerned. There was not one soldier in Caracas. Four months later the same official stated that the "anti-military system is strengthened by activity and success. It may be hard to believe that today there are not 400 armed men in all the

Republic." Officially there were supposed to be 1500 troops,
6,000 half-organized militia, and 3 small vessels and some
landing craft in the navy. By 1840 the French were also
reporting the drift of the upper class away from the regime
which was complacently practicing laissez faire. The alienated had been joining clubs and societies, including five
lodges of revived Freemasonry.[58] The United States Chargé
reported in March 1842 that the army was a "very incon-
siderable military force; yet order and the utmost security
to person and property prevail throughout the country."
Consequently, the exiled rebels were being allowed to return.[59] After 1843 the local oligarchies vainly sought to
secure severe limitations on suffrage and freedom of the
press, to enlarge the permanent army, and to obtain more
complete local control of patronage at provincial and
cantonal levels.[60]

As the end of the Páez era approached, the limitations
on the permanent army were impressive. There were in
1842–1843 roughly 1,200,000 Venezuelans and the national
government was spending 2,750,000 pesos for its operations
—slightly more than 2 pesos per capita. The authorized size
of the regular army was .0009 per cent of the population.
The armed forces were assigned about 21.5 per cent of the
budget. This is an impressive percentage made large by
the inadequacy of amounts assigned to other government
activities. The actual strength of the army, compared to its
authorized complement of 1050, was 423 officers, noncommissioned officers, and enlisted men. There were in addition
on active duty 75 officers, noncommissioned officers, and
enlisted men in cavalry militia units. The navy, besides very
meager shore installations, had one active vessel with a
complement of less than 60 men and an authorized budget

of 74,795 pesos. The army spent only 69 per cent of its budget and the navy but 55 per cent. What halcyon days for the taxpayer! Of the total army expenditures only 25 per cent went for the troops. The rest of the army's expenditures went for the courts-martial system, inactive duty and retirement pay, administration, and building maintenance. Troops were distributed in six localities with general headquarters at Maracay, the preferred residence of Páez. There were, however, 559 officers, noncommissioned officers and old soldiers of the army in retirement, on inactive duty status, or physically incapacitated.[61] The last figure was increased in 1845 by the restoration to inactive duty status of 122 officers cashiered for political difficulties from 1830 to 1836.[62] Salaries ranged downward from a relatively princely 300 pesos a month for a general-in-chief to 25 pesos for a second lieutenant and 6 pesos for a soldier. Soldiers received a 66 per cent active duty bonus and as grade increased the bonus percentage decreased, ending at 30 per cent for a captain.[63]

The elections of 1846 brought General Monágas, a "reformed" rebel of 1831 and 1835, to the presidency through the support of Páez. Monágas chose, however, to identify himself with the Liberals, rather than the Conservative supporters of Páez. The 1846 rebellion had led to the increase of the authorized strength of the permanent army to 2500 men with 1936 allotted to the infantry, 263 to cavalry, and 301 to artillery. The infantry was organized into 16 companies grouped in two battalions which were to be trained both as line companies and as light infantry. The table of organization provided a company with 4 officers, 5 sergeants, 8 corporals, 8 corporals second class, and 100 troops. There were 16 officers in the two battalion headquarters.

The artillery brigade was composed of 3 companies, each with 5 officers, 3 sergeants, 6 corporals second class, and 85 troopers. Brigade headquarters had 4 officers. The cavalry regiment was divided into 2 squadrons of 2 companies each. Regimental headquarters had 2 officers, and 1 noncommissioned officer, and each company had 3 officers, 5 sergeants, 4 corporals, 4 corporals second class, and 52 troopers. General army headquarters was authorized a complement of 11 officers. The army command was given full authority to organize and conduct necessary field operations, but authority of the commandants of arms over provincial militia units was not touched. The government claimed to be bringing the armed forces to full strength.[64]

The continuing anti-military bias of the regime, however, was clearly shown in 1849 by reduction of the regular force to less than 1000 men and by a considerable increase in appellate jurisdiction of the civil courts over courts-martial decisions.[65] Such a development greatly relieved the British Minister who had reported in 1847 that the "smallness of the amount of the military force of Venezuela hitherto, has been one of the principal causes to which she is indebted for her comparative exemption from revolutions as well as for her solvency; it is therefore with regret that I notice a growing disposition to disregard this fact and for purposes of party domination considerably to increase the permanent military force of the Republic."[66] He also indicated that financial need may have been a contributing factor to army reduction in strength in 1849, since he noted that the 1847 strength meant a tax increase or a foreign loan to pay for it.[67] Military costs for 1847–1848, three times those of 1842–1843,[68] set a rough level for the Monágas era.

The armed forces policy of the Monágas Administration

was attacked by the Conservative press as fostering militarism, replacing the rule of law with that of the sword. Conservatives opposed the "nascent military power," and denounced the abusive conduct of some militia chiefs towards civil and ecclesiastical officials.[69] Monágas had used the remaining Bolivarians as well as the Liberal Party to implement his break with the Conservatives, surrounding himself with rebels of 1831, 1835, and 1846. No wonder that some held the opinion that Monágas was imitating Bolívar's policy for the Republic of Colombia, "moulding the Republic into a military form, uniting the civil and military powers in the same hands. . . ." [70] The description of the Monágas Administration as a military system continued to be in use at the time that José Tadeo was overthrown in 1858.[71]

What the Conservatives were exercised over was the government policy towards the militia. President Monágas had actually brought the reserve militia into being in 1847 and put his own men in charge. He had disarmed the active militia because it was "composed almost entirely of landowners." [72] Monágas was using the provisions of the law to secure his control over local affairs, since the government provided the lists of names from which reserve militia units selected officers. In addition he circumvented legal requirements for appointment to other offices.[73] It is no wonder then that Conservative usage of the terms militarism and political demagoguery appeared to have much the same meaning. The Liberal press portrayed the relationship of José Tadeo Monágas and the Liberal Party in terms reminiscent of patron and client. Monágas was a "generous protector, great friend, saviour." It was a patronage to which Liberals would "know how to respond, paying with pleasure the debt which obligate[d] them since 1847 and 1848 . . ." by re-electing José Tadeo president.[74] *El Patriota* denied the charge of militarism: "You could say *military rule* if despotism had silenced the just voice of the laws; if congresses had been dissolved; if judges had lost their dignity and authority was confronted by the power of the sword that was going to replace it. You could speak of *military rule* if the precious rights of Venezuelans were silenced by terror and fear before the absolute will of a chief of arms who dictates his decisions capriciously and maintains them by bayonets. . . . You could say *military rule* if individual strength ceasing to be an integral part of social strength dominates it and takes unto itself alone the power and rights of all. . . ."[75] Liberals cited as true militarism the contemporary situation in France where the same elements of society that had so strongly opposed Charles X and Louis Philippe were silent before the military empire of Napoleon with its 500,000 troops. The Liberals rightly noted that in Venezuela "there is not even a force sufficient to keep public order."[76] Liberal opinion was justified because congress had prevented whatever substance there may have been to the charges of militarism from developing. Monágas did not enjoy unquestioned dominance after his victory over congress in 1848. That body with a change of personnel which reflected the new order of things was soon in disagreement with Monágas. It overrode his vetoes and reduced the military establishment.[77]

Both the Monágas presidents eventually recognized the difficult state of the army. At the end of his administration, José Gregorio (1851–1855) urged the congress to pass laws that would "protect military skills, that would establish true stimuli to the career, and that would make it ever noble and worthy: . . . to end abuses that kill enthusiasm and cause dismay." [78] In the following year José Tadeo commented to congress that "the army lacks a law which suitably organizes it; nor do we have a military code in harmony with our system of government." He wanted incentive *fogies* and bonuses and better retirement benefits.[79] His motives may be doubted, since everything he sought from congress would simply improve the beneficial role of a military commission as a political pension, and strengthen his position over congress. Two years later, in the face of rapidly growing discontent and obviously disillusioned in the militia, Monágas proposed a municipal guard in each province to serve as a provincial police force and as jail guards, making "possible the concentration of the veteran force in a few points, which will become centers for the formation in case of need of divisions and armies, and it will avoid the relaxation of discipline that attends the separation of soldiers and the chiefs of high rank." [80]

III

The Federal War (1859–1864), so important in other aspects, did not change the nature of the army. It did not greatly affect the authorized strength of the permanent armed forces which in 1860 was set at 3500 for the army and two steamboats with their crews for the navy. The war cost 40,000 lives and economic ruin for the nation. Victorious federalist forces rewarded themselves with over a million borrowed pesos. Compensation ranged from 150 pesos for corporals and soldiers to 8,000 for a general-in-chief plus special larger amounts for five distinguished generals.[81] The Minister of War in 1869 commented of the Federal War that the people had risen in hatred of caudillos, "hurling themselves without plan or unity into the revolution, each on his own account." [82] In 1866 it was reported that thirteen generals-in-chief, six generals of division, twelve brigadiers, nine colonels, four lieutenant colonels, three majors, four captains, and three lieutenants were given letters of compensation in the preceding year.[83]

Perhaps the most remarkable blow of the century to the institutional character of the armed forces was the Decree of June 17, 1872, which dismissed the existing army, and replaced it with three thousand-man units under chiefs appointed by and directly responsible to President Antonio Guzmán Blanco. The primary duty of these three units was to guard the three main arsenals in San Carlos, the Federal District, and Cumaná.[84] The same grave blow to institutional dignity and morale was repeated in 1877 by the new president, General Linares Alcántara, who relieved all troops on duty as of March 2. They were replaced by a new force to man the frontier posts, arsenals, naval vessels, fortresses, and garrisons.[85]

The normal costs of the permanent military establishment were increasing rapidly. The Puerto Cabello garrison in 1859 had 1,000 men in its complement at a cost of 5,000 pesos a day, or five pesos per person. In 1842–1843 the per capita cost was less than sixty cents a day. Despite increased costs, no improvements had been made in the auxiliary field services of the armed forces, and none were made during the nineteenth century.[86] Similar lack of progress was noted in the militia organization. It is true that the Minister of War in 1866 had announced in Bolivarian tones that "Venezuela has always had an army and in Venezuela we are all soldiers." [87] He should have written, "in Venezuela most of us are not even in the militia." That situation put in sharper contrast the cheapening of military rank. A career military officer of today can only be appalled on contemplating a court-martial assembled in 1872 by President and General Guzmán Blanco: twenty-three generals-in-chief, caudillos all, and political bosses of the second order; none were professional military officers.[88] The cheapening of rank was counterbalanced, perhaps, by a sharply increased pay scale. The general who had received 300 pesos a month in 1842 was earning 1440 a month in 1877. Every grade had received a spectacular increase. In percentages the pay of the soldier had been raised the most, up from 6 pesos a month to 72 pesos.[89]

An abundance of commissioned personnel did not guarantee a well-trained or numerous force. The Minister of War in 1869 commented that the government had not had a "force meriting the title of permanent. Only armed and volunteer citizens defend the present situation. . . . Governments need a permanent nucleus of forces whose organization, although decreed, has never been completed here." [90] In 1878 troops were stationed in the Federal District, La Guaira, Puerto Cabello, Ciudad Bolívar, Maturín, Goagira, and at strong points or fortresses in Maracay, Ortiz, Valencia, San Carlos de Rio Negro with nearly half the force in Caracas or within a hundred miles of the capital city.[91] However, the forces stationed in the Federal District were militia, the only organized militia units in the country.[92] In 1880 the authorized strength of the army was 2500 men, but only 2025 were on the rolls. There was in addition a supernumerary (militia) force of 2213 men called up because of rebellion in Guayana. The total military budget for the year 1880–1881 was set at 2,579,684 pesos, but actual expenditures for the year were just under 3,000,000 pesos. By mid-1881 the supernumerary force had been reduced to 1193 and the regular army numbered 2055. All officers were required to present their commissions for verification and by mid-1882 some 460 officers had presented their credentials and had been certified as properly holding their rank. Of these 258 were generals and 107 were full colonels.[93]

Annual reports of the Ministers of War and Navy reveal the state of mind in national leadership on military matters. In 1883 the minister reported failure of a "group of men who, hearkening only to the unfortunate counsels of ambition, appealed to the now discredited practice of arms to overturn a government." In reporting the new military code which modified traditional Spanish military justice, he had observed that since "no man among us is educated to be a soldier, it usually happens that he attains high rank without the knowledge that the martial laws of other nations take for granted since . . . they train the officer from childhood." [94]

After 1880 increasing emphasis was given to the training of the soldier and to his literacy. The Minister of War reported in 1883 that primary schools were functioning in the garrisons to teach recruits how to read and write, and they continued to function.[95] In tactical matters the adjustment of the Venezuelan standing army to its constant struggle with the irregular political action units of the caudillos is revealed in a report of General Francisco Rangel in 1893, which stated that General José Pacheco had dispersed his partly armed force as guerrilla groups upon learning that a superior rebel force was approaching. General Pacheco would easily adjust to mid-twentieth century Cold War partisan tactics. Rangel himself used the system of guerrillas, probably detachments of squad size since the word guerrilla also means squad, in mopping-up operations after successful combat.[96]

Despite the efforts to improve the army, the militia remained for the time being the major reliance of the national delegates "charged with mediating between local factions disputing power" in their sections of Venezuela.[97] When a rebellion was attempted in 1889 the government did not refer to the "discreditable practice of arms," but to the effort to turn back the clock to the era of "caudillism, depredations, and barbarity." [98] President Raimundo Andueza Palacios announced in 1891 that he had reorganized the army and set up a military academy to train officers in preparation for an enlarged army. He also increased the number of enlisted men and reduced that of officers in the regular infantry units.[99]

Continuing use of traditional caudillesque conciliation devices to settle political action was a constant factor operating against army morale and standards. Andueza, in the face of persistent rebellion and unpopularity, resigned, and his successor Villegas offered General Crespo, the leading figure of the rebels, a deal: an indefinite armistice, and recognition of both government and rebel forces as the armed forces of the nation. Naturally, the rebel forces would go on the government payrolls. Until congress convened, both sides would patrol Caracas and a mixed cabinet would be named and serve until a new president was chosen.[100] Crespo refused the offer and the position of the government deteriorated rapidly until Villegas fled in the face of a coup by his own commanding general, Mendoza, who then undertook a systematic milking of the financial and business community of Caracas. From August 27 to September 3, 1892, there was no government while Mendoza and his force were extracting money.[101] Mendoza fled with his loot on September 3 as Dr. Pulido took over direction of government in Caracas. Crespo defeated the forces of Pulido, who fled the city the evening of September 6, and the mob looted the city until Crespo's forces entered the city at 11 P.M.[102]

It was under President and General Crespo that greater vigor was given to the drive for professionalization of the army to provide a strong military base for power. He wanted to have in the permanent army the same degree of motivation and identification with his regime that he had found in the force he had assembled in seizing power. It involved, in fact, the professionalization of some of his own following drafted into continuing on in public service. Crespo's force for the seizure of the presidency had been assembled from guerrilla units that had "sprout[ed] like green grass on the savanna" in 1892. They were "bands of ten, of twenty, of a hundred men seeking out the *taita* [respected father figure and chief] Crespo to march behind his charger." In these units the "chiefs did not consider themselves formally commissioned and on many occasions accompanied their recruits in pillaging saloons and in cattle killing." The relationship of a unit chief with his followers was a "strange compound of agreements as among friends and of rivalry in valor." [103]

Such an elemental force can overwhelm a government and install its chief at the head of government. It can episodically create, mold, and express the consent of the governed. It cannot remain as it had been up to the moment of victory. It is exploded by its very success. Its members go home to nonpolitical activities. Its minor and intermediate chiefs become the channels of political influence and action.

Its top leadership newly installed in the control of the nation must either be content with this customary aftermath of success, or, as Crespo, seek to retain part of that force with its dedication to his personal success to contribute stability to his government. Except for its dedication to his success such a force was useless to him as it was essentially lawless, anarchic, antisocial. By combining it with the demoralized ineffective public force the president would attempt the creation of a dedicated professional military organization. Continuity of the approach is shown in official reporting.[104]

Level de Goda interpreted Crespo's desire to professionalize the armed forces as the fact of "sinister military dictatorship by . . . a most ignorant man." [105] The office of Director General of Instruction for the armed forces had been created in 1889.[106] Enforcement and supervision of garrison training were improved, and development of Venezuelan training and tactical doctrines was begun under the newly formed Grand Military Council in 1893.[107] A treatise on infantry tactics was issued as the content of the Decree of June 15, 1893.[108] Basically, it was the school of the soldier to be studied by officers so they in turn could instruct their noncommissioned officers and enlisted men. The decree also ordered an inspection after six months to verify results. A more advanced text for tactics of the infantry battalion by Colonel Siro Vásquez was adopted in 1896.[109] Both works replaced the text of the Marqués del Duero on infantry tactics adopted in 1890 and the *Cartera del soldado* added in 1891.[110] The constructive role assigned the Grand Military Council was complemented by the announced policy of drawing wartime field commanders from its members.[111]

While Crespo was undertaking what appears to have been

a real effort to improve the army, he also had to deal with the caudillos. The military commission underwent its greatest debasement, and the more important figures were rewarded at the expense of other government obligations with houses and other presents. The houses allegedly cost from fifty to seventy-five thousand dollars each.[112] Although Crespo kept his promise to call a Constitutional Convention, whose members were chosen through government influence, he became ever more unpopular because of the dictatorial character of his administration enforced through the armed force he had raised in rebellion. He rapidly rebuilt the military supplies of the government, largely from German and French sources, maintained a bodyguard of 2000 men, and enjoyed the support of the "best fighters of Venezuela, the cowboy of the Llanos." [113] He attempted to develop an effective militia so that the government could count on a maximum mobilizable force of 200,000 men.[114]

The condition of the army at the time Crespo initiated his new approach has been candidly described as undisciplined and lacking military habits since it had been formed in "rude campaign . . . full of all the crudeness of combat and permanent bivouac in which the [men] had hardly learned to handle the rifle." The regular peacetime organizational level of the army was therefore advanced from battalion to triangular regiments to maintain discipline and develop military habits through better control.[115] In 1895 the Artillery School was founded with an enrollment of all officers in garrison in the Federal District plus 54 other students admitted to the mathematics courses upon completion of primary school. At the end of the same year the army, including militia units on active duty, consisted of 10,288 officers, noncommissioned officers, and enlisted men, of whom about 1 in 17 were officers, 1 in 11 were noncommissioned officers, and 1 in 46 were noncombatants.[116] In addition to the Artillery School, officers in the Federal District were placed under an instructor to be taught their duties in the infantry.[117]

Part of Crespo's program included research in "the practices, rules, and principles which have produced the best results in other nations having a military history." To this end the Venezuelan government asked a number of foreign countries for copies of their official military publications.[118] The Venezuelan government also adhered to the Geneva Convention and gave official support to the Venezuelan Red Cross Society.[119] In July 1896 President Crespo reorganized the army. All men in the ranks with completed service terms were sent home "as an act of justice" and "in accord with law." The action was possible because some 10,000 militiamen had been mobilized in November 1895 to help dominate a rebellion. Replacements could be secured from the militia on active duty. The army was divided into three parts: a presidential guard, the army of the line, and the militia or supernumerary force on active duty. The three parts comprised 12.5 battalions of infantry, 1 squadron of cavalry, and 1 company of marines. The salary scale had declined spectacularly since 1877 to 639 Bolívars [Bs] (127.8 pesos) a month for generals, 399 (79.8 pesos) for colonels, 120 (24 pesos) for lieutenants, 55.80 (11.16 pesos) for sergeants first class, and 37.50 (7.5 pesos) for soldiers.[120]

The reorganized line army of 3600 men was considered devoted to Crespo, and as the elections of 1898 approached, the president stored 20,000 rifles at his country home for use in case of revolutionary troubles.[121] The standards of professional conduct, however, are not rapidly instilled at any time. Consequently, when the anticipated election con-

flict developed, Crespo's generals were believed to be pro-
longing the campaign in order to continue making drafts on
the treasury.[122]

In 1897 the Ministry of War and Navy submitted a plan
for a military academy, but it did not prosper.[123] The ministry attempted to win the same end by a resolution of
July 25, 1898, converting the Artillery School into a general military academy.[124] Civil conflict, however, thwarted
effective implementation of these and other measures of the
1890's and early 1900's. The problem of creating a professional effective army was appreciated, however. The army,
enlarged by mobilization to 24,000 to counter rebellion in
1899, was commanded by a variety of military and political
officials. President Andrade declared that scientific organization of the armed forces was yet to be accomplished. He
thought the task ranged "from disciplinary military education and theoretical and practical instruction, from life in
garrison and service in the field, to the laws of equal contribution of blood for all classes and for all the sons of the
fatherland; to the comparative studies and adoption of
armaments, artillery, and tactics adaptable to our customs
and to our geography of land and sea." [125] Finally in 1903
after General Cipriano Castro had twice made his claim to
the presidency effective, he decreed on July 5, 1903, a military academy, provided a budget for construction of the
buildings, and ordered classes to begin when the edifices
were completed.[126] The buildings were finished,[127] and the
academy enrolled its first class in 1910.[128] Andino success in
opening the academy may well be a product of the relative
political isolation in which Andino control of Venezuela
existed and of the consequent urgency to get on with the
task of founding a truly professional army.

Effective action towards founding a military academy

was accompanied by a stiffening of standards in the army. Following the rebellion of 1902–1903 officers on active duty were notified that they would be commissioned in accord with the new military code prepared in 1893 and issued in 1904, which based promotion on time in grade and the passing of examinations. The Minister of War and Navy subsequently observed that "it has become indispensable to be able to fulfill the duties of the rank [held] and to possess the knowledge demanded by it in order to receive the commission or title corresponding to it." [129] President and General Cipriano Castro completed the measures setting up the base for a career professional army by ending the abuse of awarding commissions to all caudillos who supported the winning side. The process was eased by the fact that Castro's had been the minority side in the civil war of 1902–1903. He owed no heavy list of obligations, although he found one or another way to honor his obligations to the Andinos. In 1904 the army was reorganized by Castro to give special emphasis to its training for small wars. The official term was *orden disperso,* equated to *sistema de guerrillas,* that is, independent action in small units.[130]

The intent of all the changes from 1893 on was to establish a career military service for officers. Moreover, the government was trying to render the two-year service in the ranks required of the single male citizen an experience useful to the nation and to the citizenry by giving the conscript civil, religious, and military instruction to end the common notion that military service debased the individual subject to it.[131] The Minister of War reported in 1909 that the abuse of retaining recruits past their two-year obligatory service was almost a thing of the past. At the same time he asked for actual and equal enforcement of the obligatory service law.[132] In the following year the same ministry demanded that the states supply from their militia units healthy unmarried recruits free of obligations that exempted them from military service.[133]

Professional career formation of the officer was the key element in the effort to reconstitute the army. His professional conduct and dedication to the support of legitimate authority would be fostered by training and by the government's refusal to commission caudillos and caciques seeking color of professional dignity for their political violence. These changes probably reflect the general modernization and improvement of armed forces in the Western world after 1890, as well as the direct experience of the Venezuelan government with the pressure of European armed forces dispatched to preserve the growing economic investment of Europeans in the course of civil conflict.

The prestige of a profession is based on the training of the men who enter it, their dedication to established ideals and observance of standards, the social importance of the service performed, and the exclusive proprietary right of its members to fulfill their professional functions. Diversion of a profession to other functions destroys its standards of preparation and service, makes its symbols common property, and opens its membership rolls to all. The Venezuelan government confronted a major task in the re-creation of the Venezuelan army, an institution reduced to inanition by long abuse. Development of a modern Venezuelan army has been in progress since 1910, building on the preliminary work begun in the 1890's.

Military careers in Venezuela at the end of the nineteenth century were discredited by three-quarters of a century of abuse of the profession's symbols and standards by political leaders who had made violence a determining element in the political process. Continuous caudillesque desecration of these symbols and standards had destroyed their validity in the eyes of the populace. Military discredit was revealed by such popular sayings as "Don't call me general! I haven't robbed anyone," [134] and by verses like this one of 1892:

> Now Venezuela does not want war
> Because this land is going to finish off
> Generals, colonels, and goldbricks
> Who do not want to work.[135]

At the same time, Gil Fortoul reported "in our days the great military men have no prestige of themselves. In peacetime those [men] are dedicated to the function of arms who cannot through some circumstance enter the liberal professions, commerce, or industry; and in times of conflict, the cultured persons that go the army start out as generals or at least as colonels, . . . and when peace returns they hastily forget or ignore such titles. In any event the disorganization of the military career had the fortunate result of making militarism impossible." [136]

As has been stated before, the rise of caudillism responded to the social destruction consequent to the war for independence. The duration of caudillism timed the profound crisis of a quasi-national community struggling to achieve its definition as a society. The inchoate, almost instinctive process of social formation had been given its goals by the Age of Democratic Revolution. These goals required reconstruction of the Venezuelan social order, development of its economy according to the principles of nineteenth-century economic liberalism, and adoption of the new representative republican political order. The empire's traditional institutional restraints on individual conduct in society had been terminated and the influence of traditional ethical principles and institutional custom were gravely weakened. New restraints had to be established, deriving their validity from the growing consensus of opinion among Venezuelans on the evils to be corrected and on the nature of the social order to be achieved. The formation of a professional career military service was only one aspect of the reconstruction of the Venezuelan social order. It was an important contribution to the elimination of caudillism.

| NOTES

CHAPTER 1:

1 Alfred Vagts, *A History of Militarism, Civilian and Military* (New York, 1959), pp. 17–20, 29–30. The general commentary on militarism is based largely on Vagts, but it has been influenced by other works cited in this chapter.

2 Vagts, pp. 21–22.

3 Vagts, p. 14.

4 Vagts, pp. 14–15, 21–22, 30–31. Vagts's views on the nature of militarism, especially on the role of the misguided civilian in arousing it, are shared by General Pedro Eugenio Aramburu, one-time Provisional President of Argentina, in his "El ejército y la democracia," *Política*, No. 6 (February 1960), pp. 37–46.

5 David C. Rapoport, "A Comparative Theory of Military and Political Types," in *Changing Patterns of Military Politics*, ed. Samuel P. Huntingdon (New York, 1962), p. 72.

6 Samuel Edward Finer, *The Man on Horseback* (New York, 1962), p. 4.

7 Finer, pp. 6–7.

8 Lyle N. McAlister, "Civil-Military Relations in Latin America," *Journal of Inter-American Studies*, III (July 1961), 341–350.

9 Magnus Mörner, "Caudillos y militares en la evolución hispano-americana," *Journal of Inter-American Studies*, II (July 1960), 295–310; Robin Humphries, "Latin America, The Caudillo Tradition," in *Soldiers and Governments*, ed. Michael Howard (London, 1957), pp. 151–165; Robert J. Alexander, "The Army in Politics," in *Government and Politics in Latin America*, ed. Harold E. Davis (New York, 1958), pp. 147–165; William S. Stokes, "Violence as a Power Factor in Latin American Politics," *Western Political Quarterly*, V (Summer 1952), 445–468; Lt. Col. Theodore Wyckoff, "The Role of the Military in Latin American Politics," *Western Political Quarterly*, XIII (September 1960), 745–763; Victor Alba, "The Stages of Militarism in Latin America," *The Role of the Military in Underdeveloped Countries*, ed. John J. Johnson (Princeton University Press, 1962), pp. 165–183; Edwin Lieuwen, "Militarism and Politics in Latin America," Johnson, *The Role*, pp. 131–163; John J. Johnson, "The Latin American Military as a Politically Competing Group in Transitional Society," Johnson, *The Role*, pp. 91–129.

10 Juan Beneyto Pérez, *Historia de la administración española ē hispanoamericana* (Madrid, 1958), pp. 291–292; José María Ots Capdequi, *Manual de historia del derecho español en las Indias y del derecho propiamente indiano* (Buenos Aires, 1945), pp. 223–229.

11 On the general subject of fuero, see pages 22–24.

12 There was an abundant legislation and regulation of military fuero, much of the essence of it being drawn together in the *Novísima recopilación de las leyes de España* of 1805. For more detailed bibliography see Chapter VI, footnotes 4, 6, and 8. See also Lyle N. McAlister, *The "Fuero Militar" in New Spain, 1764–1800* (Gainesville, Fla., 1957), pp. 5–6; and François Raymond Joseph de Pons, *Voyage à la partie oriental de la Terre-Firme dans l'Amérique méridional fait dans les années 1801, 1802, 1803, et 1804*, II (Paris, 1806), 60–61.

13 Carraccioli Parra-Pérez, *Mariño y las guerras civiles* (Madrid, 1958–60), I, 212–215; Feliciano Montenegro y Colón, *Historia de Venezuela* (Caracas, 1960), II, 117, 206; José Antonio Páez, *Autobiografía de General José Antonio Páez*, 2nd ed. (New York, 1871), II, 83–84, 253.

14 Speech of June 27, 1959, *La Religión*, Caracas, June 28, 1959.

CHAPTER 2 :

1 Laureano Vallenilla Lanz, *Disgregación y agregación*, 2nd ed. (Caracas, 1953), pp. 18, 28, 55–56, 66, 78, 81, 90–91; Carraccioli Parra-Pérez, *Historia de la primera republica de Venezuela* (Caracas, 1939), I, viii–xi; Angel César Rivas, "Orígenes de la independencia de Venezuela," in Instituto Panamericano de Geografía y Historia, *La Colonia y la inde-*

pendencia (Caracas, 1949), pp. 45–46, 50–58, 69–71, 90–96, 103–106; François Raymond Joseph de Pons, *Voyage à la partie oriental de la Terre-Firme dans l'Amérique méridional fait dans les années 1801, 1802, 1803, et 1804* (Paris, 1806), II, 39–52; Lautaro García, S. J., *Francisco de Miranda y el antiguo régimen español* (Caracas, 1961), pp. 63–72. For the documents on the evolution of the municipio in colonial Venezuela see Academia Nacional de la Historia, Mesa Redonda de la Comisión de Historia del Instituto Panamericano de Geografía e Historia, *El movimiento emancipador de hispanoamerica. Actas y ponencias* (Caracas, 1961), II, apendice documental.

2 Parra-Pérez, "Estudio preliminar," to *La constitucion federal de Venezuela de 1811*, p. 62. For comment on continuing creole resistance to measures promoting social mobility of the Negro and of mixed bloods see James F. King, "A Royalist View of the Colored Castes in the Venezuelan War of Independence," *Hispanic American Historical Review*, XXXIII, No. 4 (November 1953), 526–537.

3 Vallenilla Lanz, *Disgregación*, p. 76; Major Rafael Angarita Trujillo, "Causas y consecuencias de independencia," *Fuerzas Armadas de Venezuela*, No. 163 (January 1960), pp. 70–83; Alexander von Humboldt and A. Bonpland, *Viaje a los regiones equinocciales del nuevo continente*, ed. Lisandro Alvarado (Caracas, 1941–43), II, 332. Pedro Manuel Arcaya has enlarged on Humboldt's observations in his *Estudios sobre personas y hechos de la historia venezolana* (Caracas, 1911), pp. 127–164.

4 Pons, II, 57–59; José Sucre-Reyes, *Le système colonial espagnol dans l'ancien Venezuela* (Paris, 1939), pp. 110–113; Humboldt, III, 76–77; Augusto Mijares, "La patria de los venezolanos en 1750," in *El movimiento emancipador de hispanoamérica* (Caracas, 1961), II, 257–259; Joaquín Gabaldón Márquez, "El municipio, raiz de la república," in *El movimiento*, II, 401; Hector García Chuecos, *Relatos y comentarios sobre temas de historia venezolana* (Caracas, 1957), pp. 22–25.

5 José Manuel Restrepo, *Historia de la revolución en la República de Colombia* (Bogotá, 1942–50), VII, 300–301. The class distribution is my own very rough estimate. For population figures for the 1801–1810 period see Restrepo, III, 274, which assigned Venezuela in 1810 some 120,000 Indians, 62,000 slaves, 12,000 Spaniards, 200,000 creoles, and 406,000 mixed bloods; Francisco Javier Yanes, *Compendio de la historia de Venezuela desde su descubrimiento y conquista hasta que se declaró estado independiente* (Caracas, 1944), pp. 117–118, computed for 1801 some 138,000 whites, 270,000 Negro slaves, 276,000 freedmen and mixed bloods, and 69,000 Indians. Pons on the basis of the annual parish Lenten census gave a total of 728,000 people. He classified them as 20 per cent white, 30 per cent slaves, 40 per cent freedmen and their descendants, and 10 per cent Indians (I, 178). Restrepo based his estimates for

1810 on Humboldt (V, 108), and Yanes used Pons. Nicolás Antonio Briceño in a speech in 1811 declared that the latest carelessly taken census indicated a population of 412,857 in the Province of Caracas and 264,770 in the Provinces of Mérida, Trujillo, and Barcelona. No figures were given for Coro, Maracaibo, and Guayana. The total of 677,627 for the four most populous of the seven provinces would support the 800,000 indicated by other writers of the period, and even a higher figure if the carelessness was a significant factor in the counting ("Exposición en pro de la división de la provincia de Caracas y en defensa de Mérida y Trujillo . . . ," in *Testimonio de la época emancipadora*, p. 31). For the 1820's Humboldt estimated 766,000 in 1821 (V, 108). Francisco González Guinán, *Historia contemporánea de Venezuela* (Caracas, 1909–1925), II, 21–22, has cited a census figure of 700,000 for 1825 which he corrected to 800,000. The latter's figure for 1830 was one million. Restrepo broke down his 1825 figure of 700,000 into 26,599 Indians, 50,088 slaves, and 609,545 whites, mixed bloods and free Negroes (III, 274). Codazzi's figures for 1837–1838 indicated 221,415 Indians, three fourths of whom were classed as civilized [acculturated?] and who were probably included in Restrepo's 1825 figures under mixed bloods. Codazzi distributed the remainder of the 945,548 total population as follows: 260,000 whites, 414,151 mixed bloods, 49,782 slaves. He calculated that population losses due to war and to epidemics from 1810 to 1838 had limited the total population to two thirds of what it ought to have been (*Resúmen de la geografía de Venezuela* [Paris, 1844], p. 244).

[6] Wilson to Palmerston, No. 17, Caracas, March 4, 1842, in Great Britain, Public Record Office, Foreign Office Despatches from Venezuela, Volume 44, fol. 55v–56v (hereafter cited as FO/80/ with volume number and folios). Classification as rural or urban is mine.

[7] Editorial in *Amigo del Pueblo*, Cumana, as reprinted in *Gaceta de Gobierno*, No. 76, June 4, 1828.

[8] Eames to Cass, No. 47, Caracas, March 23, 1858, in United States, Department of State, Despatches, Venezuela, XI (hereafter cited as US/DS/V with volume number).

[9] Editorial in *Amigo del Pueblo*, reprinted in *Gaceta de Gobierno*, No. 76, June 4, 1828. The editorialist, however, assigned the cause to oppressive Spanish rule rather than to destruction of interest groups.

[10] *Gaceta de Gobierno*, No. 85, July 5, 1828.

[11] Bolívar to Juan José Flores, Barranquilla, November 9, 1830, in Federico L. Stagg y Caamaño, "El General Juan José Flores," *Boletín histórico*, No. 1 (December 1962), p. 20.

[12] Juan Beneyto Pérez, *Historia social de España y de Hispanoamérica* (Madrid, 1961), p. 385.

13 Mariano Picón-Salas, "Geografía con algunas gentes," in *Comprensión de Venezuela* (Madrid, 1955), pp. 30–31, has commented on the movement inland, the role of the major families in developing the economy of the llanos, and their service as sources of leaders during the war for independence.

14 Humboldt, V, 242–243; Eduardo Arcila Farías, "Integración de la burguesía colonial venezolana," *Política*, No. 8 (April-May 1960), pp. 66–74. There were three counts and five marqueses according to José Gil Fortoul, "El doctrinarismo y el progreso," *Pensamiento político venezolano del siglo XIX*, XIII, 173–190, esp. p. 187 (the article is Chapter V of Gil Fortoul's *El hombre y la historia*).

15 José María Ots Capdequi, *Las instituciones del Nuevo Reino de Granada al tiempo de la independencia* (Madrid, 1958), p. 111. Lautaro García has suggested the middle class character of criollismo (*Miranda*, p. 66).

16 Ramón Díaz Sánchez, "Estudio preliminar," to *Libro de actas del supremo congreso de Venezuela, 1811–1812*, pp. 42–43; James F. King, "A Royalist View of the Colored Castes in the Venezuelan War of Independence," *Hispanic American Historical Review*, XXXIII, No. 4 (November 1953), 526–537.

17 Parra-Pérez, "Estudio preliminar," to *La constitución federal de Venezuela de 1811*, p. 15; Arcila Farías, "Integración . . . ," *loc. cit.* (above, note 14). José Ladislao Andara has commented on the role of fuero as a limitation on the authority of the Captain General of Venezuela in his *Evolución social y política de Venezuela* (Caracas, 1899), p. 64.

18 Parra-Pérez, *Mariño y la independencia de Venezuela* (Madrid, 1954–56), I, 61–62. Juan Bosch has strongly stated the loyalty of the bulk of the population to the crown as a reflection of hostility to the mantuanos. He attributes the emergence of caudillism to the lower class loyalists resisting mantuano effort to reorganize politically the endangered social order ("Masas y sociedad en el año terrible de Venezuela," *Revista Nacional de Cultura*, XXII [May-August 1960], 119–127).

19 Hector García Chuecos, *Siglo dieciocho venezolano* (Caracas and Madrid, n.d.), p. 281.

20 Arcila Farías, "Integración . . . ," *loc. cit.* (above, note 14); Pons, II, 427–435.

21 García Chuecos, *Siglo dieciocho venezolano*, pp. 276–279, 296–297; Mario Briceño Iragorry reproduces a memorial of Governor Pedro Carbonnell to the crown, which analyzed the problem and declared that the triumvirate had stimulated creole-peninsular rivalry to ensure their control over Venezuelan society (*Casa León y su tiempo*, pp. 49–55). Angel Grisanti recounts Captain General Emparán's unwitting and disastrous involvement in the factional lineup in *Emparán y el golpe de estade de 1810* (Caracas, 1960), pp. 67–115.

22 Joaquín Escriche, *Diccionario razonado de legislación y jurisprudencia,* 3rd ed. (Madrid, 1847), I, 822–837; Miguel Artola, *Los orígenes de la España contemporánea* (Madrid, 1959), II, 10, 12, 22–91.

23 Pons, II, 60–61.

24 Viceroy Mendinueta to Josef Antonio Caballero, No. 1227, Santafé, September 15, 1803, and the petition of the members of his secretariat for higher pay, uniform, and *fuero de guerra,* Archivo General de Indias, Audiencia de Santafé, Legajo 628, in 27 folios.

25 Parra-Pérez, *Mariño y las guerras civiles,* I, 13; Miguel Acosta Saignes, "Los cofradías coloniales y el folklore," *Cultura universitaria,* No. 47 (January-February 1955), pp. 79–102. However, the moment of action against royal authority in 1810 saw creation of revolutionary juntas in such locales as Caracas and Cumaná with deputies representing fuero, that is classes and functional groups (Parra-Pérez, *Mariño y la independencia de Venezuela,* I, 62).

26 *Memorias del General Daniel Florencio O'Leary. Narración* (Caracas, 1952), II, 557.

27 Eloy González, *Historia de Venezuela* (Caracas, 1943–44), III, 16.

28 *La constitución federal de Venezuela de 1811,* pp. 97, 93.

29 Angarita Trujillo, p. 82; José Gil Foutoul, *Historia constitucional de Venezuela* (Berlin, 1907), II, 418–419; Williamson to Secretary of State, Caracas, June 25, 1837, in *Diplomatic Correspondence of the United States: Inter-American Affairs, 1831–1860,* XII, 541.

30 Mario Briceño Iragorry, *Ideario político* (Caracas, 1958), p. 63.

31 Nicolas E. Navarro, *La iglesia y masonería en Venezuela* (Caracas, 1928), pp. 40–44; Mary Chapman Watters, *Telón de fondo de la iglesia colonial en Venezuela . . .* (Caracas, 1951), pp. 95, 145, 161.

32 Ernesto Wolf, *Tratado de derecho constituciónal venezolano* (Caracas, 1945), I, 115–122; J. M. Hernández Ron, *Tratado elemental de derecho administrativo* (Caracas, 1945), I, 49–50, and III, 537–540, 573–593; Carlos Sánchez Espejo, *El patronato en Venezuela* (Caracas, 1953). For the struggle between Guzmán Blanco and the Catholic Church see Nicolas E. Navarro, *Anales eclesiásticos venezolanos* (Caracas, 1951), pp. 340–482, and pertinent chapters in Watters, *History of the Church in Venezuela.*

33 For an example of such diplomatic support see Lt. Gaudy Eli Giménez Rodríguez, "Visión general del bloque a Venezuela, 1902–1903," *Fuerzas Armadas de Venezuela,* No. 163 (January 1960), pp. 60–63. On the basis for British involvement see D. C. M. Pratt, "The Allied Coercion of Venezuela, 1902–1903, a Reassessment," *Inter-American Economic Affairs,* XV, No. 4, 3–28. For the length to which such support might go see J. Fred Rippy and Clyde E. Hewitt, "Cipriano Castro, 'Man Without a Coun-

try,'" *American Historical Review*, LV, No. 1 (October 1949), 36–53. See Cesar Zumeta, "Arlequín fenicio," *Pensamiento político venezolano del siglo XIX*, XIV, 60–63, for commentary on German involvement.

34 Ramón Díaz Sánchez, *Guzmán, elipse de una ambición de poder* (Caracas, 1953), pp. 187–188.

35 Bolívar to José María del Castillo y Rada, Tocuyo, August 16, 1821, *Cartas del Libertador*, XII, 241.

36 J. A. de Alamo to Bolívar, Caracas, October 7, 1825, *Epistolario de la primera república*, I, 45.

37 José Antonio Páez, *Autobiografía*, 2nd ed. (New York, 1871), II, 297; Francisco Rivas Vicuña, *Las guerras de Bolívar* (Bogotá, 1934–38), III, 65, cites the Decree of October 1, 1817, on this matter; Santander to Pedro Briceño Méndez, January 6, 1826, *Cartas y mensajes de Santander* (Bogotá, 1953–56), VI, 40–41; Santander to Montilla, January 7, 1826, *Cartas*, p. 44. In earlier comment Santander stated that some 500 persons in Apure had received land and cattle (Santander to President of Senate, March 29, 1825, *Cartas*, V, 228–229).

38 As quoted in Páez, *Autobiografía*, II, 355. Páez correctly quoted from the article in *El Venezolano*, No. 1, August 24, 1840, as reproduced in *Pensamiento político venezolano del siglo XIX*, V, 171–172. *El Venezolano* was not the first newspaper to carry comment on the disarmed condition of the state. Juan Bautista Calcaño, reportedly under the influence of General Mariano Montilla (an old Boliviano), in his editorial in *La Bandera Nacional*, No. 1, August 1, 1837, asked, "Where is the army of Venezuela?" and then stated: "Because the force authorized by Congress was not under arms, Farfán could raise the standard of rebellion and enlarge his force to the point of putting the province of Apure in danger and the whole Republic in alarm and distrust" (*Pensamiento*, X, 32). In 1839 Rafael María Baralt declared that conversation about the army was like "talking of nothing to no one." ("Lo que es un periódico," *El Correo de Caracas*, No. 4, January 30, 1839, in *Pensamiento*, X, 56). A conservative writer in *El Manzanares* of Cumaná noted that the governor had reduced the National Guard of Police to nine members and the Provincial Patrol to six. This force was useless for lack of support by other government officials (*Pensamiento*, VII, 48–49).

39 Sir Robert Ker-Porter to Jane, Caracas, April 4, 1838, Ker-Porter Papers, 27/3, pp. 73–92, esp. p. 83.

40 Wilson to Aberdeen, No. 45, Caracas, August 7, 1846, FO/80/ 39, fol. 262.

41 Briceño Iragorry, *Ideario político*, p. 62.

42 Angarita Trujillo, p. 82.

43 Vallenilla Lanz, *Cesarismo democrático. Estudios sobre las bases soci-ológicas de la constitución efectiva de Venezuela*, 3rd ed. (Caracas, 1952), pp. 110–112, 134–185, 189–190; Fermín Toro, "Discurso de 28 de Se-tiembre de 1858 . . . ," in *Reflexiones sobre la ley de 10 de abril de 1834 y otras obras* (Caracas, 1941), pp. 298–299, 305, and "Reflexiones sobre la ley de 10 de abril . . . ," in *Reflexiones*, pp. 16, 102–103, 153–154; Briceño Iragorry, *Ideario político*, pp. 55–62; Dr. Laureano Villanueva, *Vida del valiente ciudadano General Ezequiel Zamora* (Caracas, 1898), pp. 17–18; Mariano Picón-Salas, "Antitesis y tesis de nuestra historia," in *Comprensión de Venezuela* (Madrid, 1955), pp. 181–183; Francisco Javier, Jr., "Epistolas catilinarias. Cuarta," *Pensamiento político vene-zolano del siglo XIX*, XII, 54–77, esp. pp. 67–68.

44 Ramon Espejo to the Vice-president, Caracas, July 17, 1821, and Juan José Rivas Pacheco to the Intendant, Caracas, September 27, 1821, in Archivo Nacional de Colombia, Solicitudes, XVI, fol. 250–250bis, 561–561bis.

45 Vallenilla Lanz, *Cesarismo*, p. 112.

46 Parra-Pérez, *Marino y las guerras civiles*, I, 178. No study of the gamonal has been made. The evaluation presented here is a summary of impres-sions received from Colombian and Venezuelan sources in which the gamonal is referred to but not studied.

47 Ambrosio Oropeza, "El estado constitucional venezolano desde 1830 hasta 1870," *Política*, No. 19 (December 1961), pp. 13–33.

48 The commentary on caciquismo has been made against the background of the Spanish version described in Marcelo Martínez Alcubilla, *Dic-cionario de la administración española*, II, 5, and in Ateneo Científico, y Literario y Artistico de Madrid, *Oligarquía y caciquismo como la forma actual de gobierno en España, urgencia y modo de cambiarla*, especially the introductory essay by Joaquín Costa, pp. 11–111, in which past analyses of caciquismo are reviewed.

49 Virgilio Tosta, *F. Tosta García* (Caracas, 1954), p. 68.

50 See below, Chapter 3, esp. pp. 47, 50–52, 57, 59.

51 Santander to President of Senate, Bogotá, June 29, 1824, *Cartas y men-sages*, IV, 486.

52 Bolívar to Convención de Ocaña, Bogotá, February 29, 1828, in *Gaceta de Gobierno*, No. 71, May 17, 1828.

53 Lovera to Intendant, Chacao, September 13, 1821, Archivo Nacional de Colombia, Solicitudes, XVI, fol. 130–131.

54 Secretary of Interior José Manuel Restrepo to Intendant of Department of Venezuela, Bogotá, April 16, 1828, *Gaceta de Gobierno*, No. 74, May 28, 1828.

⁵⁵ Editorial article, *Gaceta de Gobierno*, No. 86, July 8, 1828; Decree of August 16, 1827, in *Gaceta de Gabierno*, No. 26, December 12, 1827; Rafael María Baralt and Ramón Díaz, *Resumen de la historia de Venezuela desde . . . 1797 hasta 1830* (Bruges and Paris, 1939), II, 306.

⁵⁶ *Gaceta de Gobierno*, No. 106, September 17, 1828. Páez presided and the views of the delegates coincided with his.

⁵⁷ *Gaceta de Gobierno*.

⁵⁸ *Gaceta de Gobierno*, No. 113, October 8, 1828.

⁵⁹ Feliciano Montenegro y Colón, *Historia de Venezuela* (Caracas, 1952), II, 160–161.

⁶⁰ For the law organizing local government in 1830 see *Cuerpo de leyes de Venezuela . . . 1830 hasta 1850* (Caracas, 1851), pp. 57–63, and its amendments in 1839 (pp. 314–322) and 1841 (p. 485)—hereafter cited as *Cuerpo de leyes;* Fermín Toro, pp. 301–303; González Guinán, II, 182, 467.

⁶¹ *Cuerpo de leyes*, p. 772.

⁶² Vicente Lecuna, *La revolución de Queipa*, pp. 36–37, 54, 59.

⁶³ *Gaceta de Venezuela*, Nos. 668, 669, 671, and 716 of 1844, 763 of 1845, and 824 of 1846. On the encysted loneliness of life in the llanos see John Mayer, "El llanero," *The Atlantic Monthly . . .*, III (1859), 174–188. On the organization and functioning of a hato see Carlos Siso, *La formación del pueblo venezolano* (New York, 1941), fn. pp. 328–329.

⁶⁴ Humboldt, II, 308.

⁶⁵ Rivas Vicuña, III, 26.

⁶⁶ Domingo Faustino Sarmiento, *Facundo: civilización y barbarie*, p. 38.

⁶⁷ *La Patriota*, February 7, 1852.

⁶⁸ *La Prensa*, March 16, 1847.

⁶⁹ *Historia institucional de Argentina*, p. 140. See Siso's brief commentary on the llanero caudillos and their followers, pp. 337–338.

⁷⁰ Rivas Vicuña, III, 58–59.

⁷¹ Joaquín Gabaldón Márquez states that caudillesque anarchy "stifled all possibility of social progress in the midst of the dispersed multitudes. Our country was, then, in effect no more than a group of a few cities, of minority population, seat and immediate dominion of caudillos and caciques, surrounded by the scattered rural multitudes, apt only to be the object of economic, political, and military exploitation by that new kind of feudal lords." ("Enlace de las generaciones," in *Historia de la historiografía venezolana*, ed. Germán Carrera Damas [Caracas, 1961], p. 187).

[72] FO/80/114, fol. 150–152r. Outgoing President José Gregorio Monágas admitted much of this in his message to congress on January 20, 1855 (see broadside enclosed with Eames to Marcy, No. 7, Caracas, February 11, 1855, US/DS/V/X), as did Provisional President Julian Castro in his address to the deputies of the Great Convention, Caracas, July 5, 1858 (enclosure to Eames to Cass, No. 60, Caracas, July 14, 1858, *ibid.*, XI).

[73] FO/80/114, fol. 152v–154r.

[74] Williamson to Secretary of State, No. 28, Caracas, June 25, 1837; Hall to Secretary of State, No. 36, Caracas, May 25, 1844; and No. 43, October 28, 1844; Shields to Buchanan, No. 48, Caracas, January 29, 1848, US/DS/V/I, II, IV.

[75] Díaz Sánchez, *Guzmán*, pp. 375–378; Parra-Pérez, *Mariño y las guerras civiles*, I, 135–144; Minister of Foreign Affairs Juan Manuel Manrique to Secretary of State, Caracas, May 17, 1844, enclosure to Hall to Secretary of State, May 23, 1844, and Hall's despatches of May 23 and October 28, 1844, and Turpin to Secretary of State, July 1, 1859, in *Diplomatic Correspondence of the United States* . . . , XII, 545–548, 825.

[76] Leonce Levraud to Minister of Justice Gutiérrez, Caracas, June 10, 1856, from a copy in FO/80/116, fol. 243v–247.

[77] Díaz Sánchez, *Guzmán*, pp. 377, 522.

[78] Orme to Russell, No. 26, Caracas, September 22, 1859, FO/80/139, fol. 173.

[79] Pedro Arcaya, "Federación y democracia en Venezuela," *Estudios sobre personas*, pp. 169–198.

[80] Mathison to Middleton, Ciudad Bolívar, April 15, 1872, FO/80/211, fol. 316.

[81] Stillwell to Seward, Caracas, No. 6 (December 26, 1867), No. 11 (February 6, 1868), No. 34 (May 27, 1868), and Erastus C. Pruyn to Seward, No. 31 (September 21, 1868), No. 44 (October 30, 1868), in *House Executive Documents, 40th Congress, 3rd Session*, Part II, pp. 933, 936–937, 942–943, 971, 980. These despatches are supported by the observations of the distinguished Cecilio Acosta who believed a prosperous peace a much more effective solvent of the old order. Acosta classified the states as "feudal petrifications," strongholds impervious to violence, and therefore a solid base for local interest and for those resisting change ("Tullius a Clodius," No. 1, December 16, 1867, in *Pensamiento político venezolano del siglo XIX*, IX, 199–200. Acosta's views were also those of Dr. Rafael Villavicencio expressed in a paper read at his admission to the Academia Nacional de la Historia of Venezuela in 1900. Villavicencio stated that the Constitution of 1864 divided the nation, "not into independent entities joined by a federal pact and governed by republican

laws, but into true feudal jurisdictions, commanded by chiefs, absolute in their district, but submitted to the nominal power of the Supreme Chief who resided in the capital. . . . It was on a small scale analogous to Europe after the dismemberment of the empire of Charlemagne." (*Pensamiento político venezolano del siglo XIX*, XIII, 98–99).

[82] Pruyn to Seward, No. 44, Caracas, October 30, 1868, *House Executive Documents, 40th Congress, 3rd Session*, Part II, pp. 980–981.

[83] Middleton to Darby, Caracas, July 2, 1877, FO/80/248, fol. 8.

[84] Cedeño to Urbaneja, Valencia, October 27, 1881, "Documento inédito," *Boletín del Archivo Histórico de Miraflores*, No. 6 (May-June 1960), 11–16, esp. p. 13.

[85] Andara, *Evolución social*, p. 49.

[86] Loomis to Sherman, No. 75, Caracas, February 9, 1898, US/DS/V/ XLVIII.

[87] Press clippings enclosed in Loomis to Hay, No. 433, Caracas, May 3, 1900, US/DS/V/LI.

[88] Loomis to Hay, No. 385, Caracas, January 20, 1900, US/DS/V/L.

[89] Presbyterian Missionary T. S. Pond to Bowen, Caracas, August 23, 1902, enclosure to Bowen to Hay, No. 120, Caracas, August 24, 1902, US/DS/V/LV.

[90] Fernando González, *Mi compadre* (Barcelona, 1934), p. 48.

[91] González Guinán, II, 464–465.

[92] Middleton to Granville, No. 12, Caracas, June 8, 1872, in FO/80/211, fol. 308–311r.

[93] See pertinent decrees and resolutions in *Recopilación de leyes y decretos de Venezuela*, V, 128–129, XII, 376, 496, XIV, 323, XVI, 263, XVII, 63; and *Memoria que dirige al congreso de los Estados Unidos de Venezuela el ministro de Guerra y Marina en 1894* (hereafter cited as *Memoria* with year. Prior to 1889 as *Exposición* and year), I, 221–222, *Memoria . . . 1897*, Document 9, and *Memoria . . . 1899*, I, xxx.

CHAPTER 3:

[1] Virgilio Tosta, *El caudillismo según once autores venezolanos* (Caracas, 1954), pp. 9–12, 18.

[2] Laureano Vallenilla Lanz, *Cesarismo democratico. Estudios sobre . . . ,* 3rd ed. (Caracas, 1952), pp. 175–176.

[3] Mario Briceño Iragorry, *Ideario político* (Caracas, 1958), p. 72.

[4] Francisco González de Linares and Pedro Mijares to Secretary of State

and Despatch of Government of Ultramar, Madrid, June 26, 1821, in Hector García Chuecos, *Historia documental de Venezuela* (Caracas, 1957), pp. 129–133.

5 Fernando Rivas Vicuña, *Las guerras de Bolívar* (Bogotá, 1934–38), III, 161.

6 Santander to Governor of the Province, Guanapalo, December 8, 1818, in *Cartas y mensajes*, I, 109.

7 Mario Briceño Perozo, "Estudio preliminar," to *Causas de infidencia* (Caracas, 1960), I, 31–39.

8 Rivas Vicuña, III, 32.

9 Fermín Toro, *Reflexiones sobre la ley de 10 abril de 1834 y otras obras* (Caracas, 1941), p. 262.

10 Ramón Díaz Sánchez, *Guzmán, elipse de una ambición de poder* (Caracas, 1953), p. 149; A. M. Soteldo, "Voto Salvado," Caracas, March 20, 1847, in *La Prensa*, No. 43, March 23, 1847.

11 Beneyto Pérez, *Historia social de España y de Hispanoamérica* (Madrid, 1961), pp. 381–386.

12 Díaz Sánchez, *Guzmán*, p. 169.

13 Manuel Antonio Pulido Méndez, *Régulo Olivares y su época* (Mexico, 1954), p. 52.

14 Díaz Sánchez, *Guzmán*, pp. 553–554.

15 Wilson to Palmerston, No. 30, Caracas, March 21, 1848, FO/80/55, fol. 85v.

16 James Barnes, "A Glimpse at Venezuelan Politics," *The Outlook*, LXXIII (1903), 479–483.

17 Militia Law of 1854, *La Patriota*, May 6, 1854.

18 Mariano Picón-Salas, *Los dias de Cipriano Castro (historia venezolana del 1900)*, 2nd ed. (Barquisimeto, 1955), pp. 10–11.

19 José Ladislao Andara, "En defensa de la causa liberal," Curaçao, November 9, 1903, in *De política e historia* (Caracas, 1899), pp. 53–54.

20 The role of the urban sector in caudillism was more important after 1870 than before, reflecting the greatly increased role of public services and raw material exploitation in the economy. Cecilio Acosta observed in 1867 that the educated elements were to blame for the generalized disorder because they refused to carry over into direct political action their socioeconomic leadership of Venezuelan society. He blamed them because his study of politics in the Western world taught him that after achieving its goal in violent political action the urban upper-class element returned to its economic and professional interests. His observation of twenty years of disorder in Venezuela led him to state that "agitation finds

in the rural areas its bivouacs and recruits." (Tullius a Clodius, No. 1, December 16, 1867, *Pensamiento político venezolano del siglo XIX*, IX, 196–198.)

21 Lt. Col. Manuel Moran, "Los multitudes y la tropa. Fragmentos del curso de educación moral," *Revista del Ejército, Marina y Aeronaútica*, XIII (August 1937), 43–48.

22 Prologue to José Carrillo Moreno, *Matías Salazar. Historia venezolana* (Caracas, 1954), p. x.

23 Vallenilla Lanz, *Cesarismo*, p. 115.

24 Briceño Iragorry, *Ideario político*, p. 66.

25 Andrés Level de Goda, *Historia contemporánea de Venezuela política y militar (1858–1886)* (Barcelona, 1893), p. 557.

26 Caraccioli Parra-Pérez, *La monarquía en la Gran Colombia* (Madrid, 1957), p. 61.

27 Williamson to Secretary of State, Caracas, June 25, 1837, in *Diplomatic Correspondence of the United States . . .* , XII, 541.

28 Editorial in *Política*, No. 6 (February 1960), p. 8. For a brief treatment of Venezuelan political parties in the nineteenth century see Manuel Vicente Magallanes, *Partidos políticos venezolanos* (Caracas, 1959), pp. 25–60.

29 As quoted in Tosta, *El caudillismo*, p. 14. Rafael Fernando Seijas has blueprinted in his *El Presidente* the reality, tactics, and reach of presidential authority under the despotic caudillo. First published in 1891, reprinted in 1940, the work is available in *Pensamiento político venezolano del siglo XIX*, XI, 89–156.

30 As quoted in Díaz Sánchez, *Guzmán*, p. 221.

31 Middleton to Earl of Derby, Caracas, February 2, 1877, FO/80/247, fol. 93r–94v. General Linares Alcántara upon becoming president promptly persuaded congress to award defeated candidate Zavarse 20,000 pesos because of his past services to Federation and Regeneration, his private difficulties, and the popular support he enjoyed in some of the states of the union (Decree of April 3, 1877, in *Recopilación*, VII, 495–496).

32 As quoted in Vicente Lecuna, *La revolución de Queipa* (Caracas, 1954), p. 19.

33 Lecuna, p. 18.

34 George Wise, *El caudillo. A portrait of Antonio Guzmán Blanco* (New York, 1951), p. 125.

35 Santiago Briceño Ayestarán, *Memorias de su vida militar y política . . .* (Caracas, 1948), pp. 5, 30.

36 Rafael Cayama Martínez, *El General Gregorio Segundo Riera. Notas biográficas* (Caracas, 1941), pp. 41, 47.

37 Briceño Ayestarán, pp. 31–37; Col. Tomás Pérez Tenreiro, "Cipriano Castro, ensayo de interpretación militar," *Fuerzas Armadas de Venezuela*, No. 158–159 (August-September 1959), pp. 14–22. See also Ramon J. Velásquez's introductory study to General Antonio Paredes, *Como llegó Cipriano Castro al poder* (Caracas, 1954), for supporting commentary on Venezuelan political parties (pp. cvi-cx).

38 Lecuna, *Queipa*, p. 23.

39 Beneyto Pérez, *Historia social*, p. 386; José Carrillo Moreno, *Matías Salazar. Historia venezolana*, p. x. Large scale foreign investments were facilitated by Guzmán Blanco (Wise, pp. 87–88, 100, 105–106), who insisted on treatment as a full equal by foreign governments (Díaz Sánchez, *Guzmán*, p. 546).

40 A decision of legislative or of administrative nature arrived at in formal meeting of an audiencia and viceroy.

41 Miguel Blanco Herrero has dealt with this practice in his *Política de España en Ultramar* (Madrid, 1888), pp. 565–566.

42 Santander to Senate and House, Bogotá, April 17, 1823, *Cartas y mensajes*, IV, 86–94, esp. p. 93. Santander agreed with bourgeois opinion in pre-revolutionary eighteenth century France (Vagts, *A History*, rev. ed. [New York, 1959], pp. 76–77).

43 José María Ots Capdequi, *Las Instituciones del Nuevo Reino de Granada al tiempo de la independencia* (Madrid, 1958), p. 33.

44 Wise, pp. 164–173.

45 Pedro Maria Morantes, *Los felicitadores* (Caracas, 1952).

46 Middleton to Derby, Caracas, February 19, 1877, FO/80/247, fol. 122–124.

47 Picón-Salas, "Proceso del pensamiento venezolano," in *Comprensión*, p. 141. Despite the subservient role imposed on them, the mental baggage of the nineteenth century Venezuelan intellectuals was impressive (William Whatly Pierson, "Foreign Influences on Venezuelan Political Thought, 1830–1930," *Hispanic American Historical Review*, XV, No. 1 [February 1934], 3–42).

48 For the title see Decree of May 20, 1877, in *Recopilación*, VII, 504, and for the money see Decree of April 4, 1878, in *Recopilación*, VII, 544.

49 Loomis to Sherman, No. 32, Caracas, November 5, 1897, US/DS/V/XLVII.

50 Luis Jerónimo Alfonzo has asserted that Mónagas used military grades and other favors to buy support for his administration (*Breve analisis del pasado de Venezuela* [Caracas, 1872], p. 13). In 1883 the title of General-in-Chief was made honorific, granted by congress. Subsequent military lists distinguished between those created by congress as an honor and

those previously commissioned by presidents. The history of the rank was reviewed in the *Memoria* of the Ministry of War and Navy of 1910 which reported a total of 175 so commissioned between 1812 and 1893. Of these 11 were named from 1812 to 1825, during the war for independence; 4 were appointed by congress from 1854 to 1859, 1 by Páez in 1863, 1 by the Federal Assembly in 1863, 106 by General Falcón during the Federal War from 1859 to 1864, 1 by José Tadeo Monágas in 1868, 25 by Guzmán Blanco from 1870 to 1877, 4 by congress in 1880, and 22 by constituent assembly in 1893 at the request of General Joaquín Crespo.

51 *Exposición* . . . *1857*, pp. 77–88.

52 Andara, *La Evolución social y política de Venezuela* (Caracas, 1899), p. 49.

53 Andres Vigas, *Perfiles parlementarias* (Caracas, 1893), pp. 65–66.

54 See Chapter 7.

55 Pérez Tenreiro, pp. 14–22 (above, note 37). That development would invalidate in the future a current statement on the outbreak of the rebellion of 1902: "With difficulty one can find as many as twelve names of those who can effectively induce anarchy in the land, and around whom are focused in kaleidoscopic groups a scant thousand parish caciques. It is that minority which decides peace or war." (Cesar Zumeta, "La ley de cabestro," *Pensamiento político venezolano del siglo XIX*, XIV, 48–60, esp. p. 55).

56 Zoila Vidal to Juan Vicente Gómez, Cumaná, November 10 and December 7 and 23, 1909, "Los caudillos de Oriente y las elecciones de 1909," *Boletín del Archivo Histórico de Miraflores*, II, No. 7 (July–August 1960), 21–22, 31–33, 36–37.

CHAPTER 4:

1 Rafael Bolívar Coronado, *El llanero* (Madrid, 1919), pp. 40, 126–143; Alexander von Humboldt and A. Bonpland, *Viaje a los regiones equinocriles del nuevo continente*, ed. by Lisandro Alvarado (Caracas, 1941–43), III, 239.

2 Representación del Colonel D. Fernández Mijares, Commandante Política y Militar de Barinas, February 14, 1794 (copy of 1798), in Archivo General de Indias, Audiencia de Santafé, Legajo 582.

3 Humboldt, V, 43.

4 Hector García Chuecos, *Siglo dieciocho venezolano* (Caracas and Madrid, n.d.), p. 336.

5 Juan Buscat, "Prospecto de mejora para la ciudad de Barcelona," *Causas de infidencia*, I, 446–449.

6 Bolívar Coronado, pp. 126–143. Páez did not mention these events in his autobiography.

7 Fernando Rivas Vicuña has dealt with the development of guerrilla leaders and their forces from 1814–17 in *Las guerras de Bolívar* (Bogotá, 1934–38), II, 88–101, 190–191, and III, 59–60, 161–162.

8 Major Rafael Angarita Trujillo, "Causas y consecuencias de independencia," *Fuerzas Armadas de Venezuela*, No. 163 (January 1960), p. 81.

9 Ramon Díaz Sánchez, *Guzmán, elipse de una ambición de poder* (Caracas, 1953), p. 14.

10 Jose Manuel Restrepo, *Diario político y militar* . . . (Bogotá, 1954), I, 263, 269, 298–299, 331; Caraccioli Parra-Pérez, *Mariño y la independencia de Venezuela* (Caracas, 1954–56), IV, 11–18, 328, 390. Páez had reported early in 1823 that "as soon as a faction is destroyed in one place and the department in apparent peace, immediately another one appears: here a movement, there a party, and to silence them and impose law on these strong spirits it is always necessary to keep a strong army in sight." (Páez to Secretary of War, Puerto Cabello, February 11, 1823, in *Archivo del General José Antonio Páez* [Bogotá, 1939–1957], II, 158–159). To keep that strong visible army, Páez requested that he be sent replacements from other departments since "in Venezuela it is absolutely impossible to keep a recruit in the ranks. . . . These men, near family and homes are deserting after 8 to 10 months of rigorous enclosure." (Páez to Secretary of War, Paso Real, November 2, 1823, in *Archivo*, pp. 245–246).

11 *Gaceta de Gobierno*, October 27, 1827, and March 22, April 19, April 22, and August 13, 1828.

12 *Gaceta de Gobierno*, December 8, 1827.

13 Restrepo, Diario, I, 325, 338, 344, 367, 371, 372; Parra-Pérez, *Mariño y la independencia*, IV, 399–401.

14 For example, see Joaquín Gabaldón Márquez, "El enlace de las generaciones," in *Historia de la historiografía venezolana* (Caracas, 1961), pp. 185–186.

15 Laureano Vallenilla Lanz, *Cesarismo democrático* (Caracas, 1952), p. 185. Tomás Lander reported in 1833 the reconstitution of the mounted patrols set up in 1827 to enforce orders of the jefe político of canton and of the courts. Calabozo Cantón got the first one and other cantons of the Province of Caracas had to wait on the availability of funds (*Pensamiento político venezolano del siglo XIX*, IV, 203).

16 José Carrillo Moreno, *Matías Salazar. Historia venezolana* (Caracas, 1954), pp. 22–23.

17 Fernando Gonzáles, *Mi compadre* (Barcelona, 1934), p. 16.

18 Parra-Pérez, *Mariño y las guerras civiles*, I, 187, 205–206, 212–215, 240, 247, II, 128–129; Díaz Sánchez, *Guzmán*, pp. 182–201; Francisco Tosta García, *El poder civil. Episodios venezolanos. Segunde serie* (Caracas, 1911), pp. 15–24.

19 Lt. Col. Gilmore Gregg to Wellington, Kingston, September 13, 1835, FO/80/1, fol. 123r–124r.

20 Rafael María Baralt and Ramón Diaz, *Resumen de la historia de Venezuela desde . . . 1797 hasta 1830* (Bruges and Paris, 1939), II, 431.

21 G. F. Hill to My Lord, Trinidad, September 28, 1835, FO/80/1, fol. 190–193. Hill's analysis was confirmed by Restrepo, *Diario*, III, 29, and by Francisco Javier Yanes, Jr., in the first of his *Epistolas Catilinarias* [1835], reprinted in *Pensamiento político venezolano del siglo XIX*, XII, 21–76, esp. pp. 21–27.

22 Tomás Michelena, *Reseña biográfica de Santos Michelena*, 2nd ed. (Caracas, 1951), pp. 110–116.

23 On the political benefits of exile see Williamson to Secretary of State, No. 22, Caracas, October 8, 1836, US/DS/V/I.

24 Parra-Pérez, *Mariño y las guerras civiles*, II, preface. Liberal analysis of the 1830–1836 period distinguished a beneficent period which ended in 1834 with the Law of April 10 on liberty of contracts which it alleged opened an era of oligarchic conquest and oppression of society. Liberal commentary on the effects of that law were an early nationalist cry against the surrender of financial control of the economy to foreign lenders. The outcome of the War of the Reforms simplified the oligarchy's takeover. A consistent erosion of public and individual liberties after 1836 was charged, until at last the regime was terminated by rebellion and by the Monágas (Felipe Larrazabal, "Ojeada histórico-política sobre Venezuela en los catorce años de su administración constitucional," *El Venezolano*, No. 264, December 10, 1844, in *Pensamiento político venezolano del siglo XIX*, X, 293–304).

25 Sir Robert Ker-Porter to Jane, Caracas, January 14 and February 10, 1839, in Ker-Porter Papers, 28/5, p. 17.

26 Parra-Pérez, *Mariño y las guerras civiles*, II, 13, 74–75.

27 An example is the 1869 manifesto of Vicente Amengual in Carlos Felice Cardot, *Antología cabudareña* (Barquisimeto, May 1, 1944), pp. 13–23.

28 Wilson to Palmerston, No. 50, Caracas, August 21, 1846, FO/80/39, fol. 322–324. The same theme is further developed in a despatch of May 20, 1847, FO/80/45, fol. 156–158.

29 Dr. Laureano Villanueva, *Vida del valiente ciudadano general Ezequiel Zamora* (Caracas, 1898), p. 83.

30 Díaz Sánchez, *Guzmán*, pp. 306–307, 329, 331.

[31] Wilson to Palmerston, Caracas, February 4, 1847, FO/80/44, fol. 84–86.

[32] Díaz Sánchez, *Guzmán*, p. 259. See also the statement of President Carlos Soublette to Congress in *Gaceta de Venezuela*, No. 671, January 28, 1844, and a congressional report on the "Malestar de la agricultura," *Gaceta de Venezuela*, No. 704, September 15, 1844. Francisco Aranda in "Un pensamiento para ser examinado," reported the details of usurious interest rates in 1844 (*Pensamiento político venezolano del siglo XIX*, XII, 414–433).

[33] H. Bedford Wilson, "A General Review of the Trade of Venezuela during the Financial Year ending the 30th of June 1845," Caracas, March 31, 1845, FO/80/34, fol. 79–81. Juan Vicente González in the first of his eleven letters from *Cicerón a Catilina* (November 22, 1845, to April 24, 1846) wrote: Broken and exhausted, that porkbarrel oligarchy still struggles to maintain itself on the land and even thinks itself victorious because it clutches in its bloody hands the iniquitous laws that have impoverished the country and through which it threatens to convert [Venezuela] into a lucrative fief or into a fearsome solitude." (*Pensamiento político venezolano del siglo XIX*, II, 310.)

[34] Wilson to Aberdeen, No. 26, Caracas, June 1, 1846, FO/80/39, fol. 1–5.

[35] Díaz Sánchez, *Guzmán*, pp. 303, 329.

[36] José Aniceto Serrano, *Violencia ejercida por el poder ejecutivo de la República de la Venezuela en 1848* . . . , as quoted in Tomás Michelena, *Resumen de la vida militar y política del ciudadano esclarecido General José Antonio Páez* (Caracas, 1890), pp. 127–128. On the same points see Restrepo, *Diario*, III, 389, who noted a rising criminal rate and the calling up of a thousand militiamen to repress criminal gangs in 1844. United States Chargé Hall reported their cries of "Liberty Forever" and "Death to the Oligarchy" (No. 36, Caracas, June 27, 1844, US/DS/V/II) and later reflected Serrano's opinion but included racial conflict (No. 43, Caracas, October 28, 1844, US/DS/V/II). Juan Vicente González attacked in *Diario de la Tarde* in 1846 the Liberal Party approach to gaining political power (No. 2), but did note the party's well-thought-out plan which he attributed to Guzmán (No. 3). In an editorial in No. 125 he stated: "Guzmán is preaching social revolution. He has declared the proprietor, the hardworking man, a tyrant over the lazy and the vagrant; he calls on these to destroy the Republic and in exchange for their votes he offers them the wealth and the social position and the heads of whoever counts." He concluded by stating that conspiracy was regarded as a constitutional right. (*Pensamiento político venezolano del siglo XIX*, III, 53–55, 114–115.)

[37] *El Liberal*, No. 615, September 12, 1846, enclosure to Shields to Buchanan, No. 25, Caracas, September 30, 1846, US/DS/V/III. For similar

developments in adjacent Nueva Granada see Robert L. Gilmore, "Nueva Granada's Socialist Mirage," *Hispanic American Historical Review*, XXXVI (May 1956), 190–210.

38 Wilson to Palmerston, February 4, 1848, FO/80/54, fol. 143–153.

39 Parra-Pérez, *Mariño y las guerras civiles*, III, preface.

40 "Translation of a letter addressed by a distinguished individual [Veritas] in Caracas to a friend at St. Thomas," October 5, 1856, FO/80/117, fol. 215–229.

41 Virgilio Tosta, *El caudillismo* . . . (Caracas, 1954), p. 18.

42 Andrés Level de Goda, *Historia contemporanea de Venezuela política y militar (1858–1886)* (Barcelona, 1893), pp. 109–110.

43 Turpin to Cass, No. 13, Caracas, April 12, 1859, US/DS/V/XII.

44 Turpin to Cass, No. 15, Caracas, May 6, 1859, *ibid*.

45 Turpin to Cass, Nos. 16, 17, and 18, Caracas, July 1, July 25, and September 7, 1859, *ibid*.

46 Turpin to Cass, No. 24, Caracas, January 20, 1860, *ibid*.

47 Turpin to Cass, Nos. 33 and 39, August 24 and October 25, 1860, *ibid*.

48 Culver to Seward, No. 2, Caracas, October 8, 1862, *ibid*., XIII.

49 Culver to Seward, Nos. 21, 23, 24, and 26, Caracas, May 1, May 19, June 10, and June 24, 1863, *ibid*.

50 As quoted in Tosta, *El caudillismo*, pp. 18–19.

51 Level de Goda, pp. xvii-xviii.

52 Ildefonso Riera Aguinagalde, *Páginas escogidas* (Barquisimeto, 1951), pp. 37–46.

53 Díaz Sánchez, *Guzmán*, p. 522.

54 Middleton to Granville, No. 48, Caracas, July 8, 1872, FO/80/212, fol. 10, 14–15.

55 Santiago Briceño Ayestarán, *Memorias de su vida militar y política* . . . (Caracas, 1948), p. 13.

56 Briceño Ayestarán, p. 19. According to Arturo Croce such "so-called campaigns were uprisings of a few days or months. They did not exceed assault on a village or caserio, then withdrawal to work, to the mountains, or to exile in Colombia" (*Francisco Croce, un general civilista* [Caracas, 1959], p. 28).

57 Briceño Ayestarán, p. 28.

58 Lecuña, *Queipa*, pp. 60–75.

59 Loomis to Hay, No. 341, Caracas, November 1, 1899, US/DS/V/L.

60 Loomis to Hay, No. 346, Caracas, November 7, 1899, *ibid.*

61 Loomis to Hay, Nos. 385 and 407, Caracas, January 20 and March 22, 1900, *ibid.*

CHAPTER 5:

1 Ramón Escobar Salom, "Estudio preliminar," to Francisco Javier Yanes, *Manual político del venezolano* (Caracas, 1959), pp. 13–14.

2 Feliciano Montenegro y Colón, *Historia de Venezuela* (Caracas, 1960), II, 117, 206.

3 Dr. Laureano Villanueva, *Vida del valiente ciudadano general Ezequiel Zamora* (Caracas, 1898), pp. 7–13, 83–84, 101–103, 119–130, 155, 220, 224, 234, 240–247.

4 Jacinto R. Pachano, *Biografía del mariscal Juan C. Falcón* (Paris, 1876), pp. 3–26, 452.

5 José Carillo Moreno, *Matías Salazar Historia venezolana* (Caracas, 1954), pp. ix, 3–4, 11–17, 24–29, 33, 45, 48, 59, 67, 79, 86, 92–96, 105; Ramón Díaz Sánchez, *Guzmán, elipse de una ambición de poder* (Caracas, 1953), p. 553.

6 Virgilio Tosta, *F. Tosta García* (Caracas, 1953), pp. 28–29.

7 On Guzmán Blanco's life see Díaz Sánchez, *Guzmán;* George Wise, *El Caudillo. A Portrait of Antonio Guzmán Blanco* (New York, 1951); Manuel Briceño, *Los ilustres ó la estafa de los Guzmanes* (Caracas, 195–).

8 William A. Pile to Fish, No. 80, Caracas, May 7, 1873, in *House Executive Documents, 43rd Congress, 1st Session, 1873–1874,* II, 1171–1172; Middleton to Derby, Caracas, February 2, 1877, FO/80/247, fol. 93r.

9 Manuel Modesto Gallegos, *Anales contemporáneos. Memorias del General Manuel Modesto Gallegos, 1925* (Caracas, 1925).

10 Juan A. Lossada Piñeres, *Hombres notables de la revolución del 92 en Venezuela* (Caracas, 1893), II, 13–50.

11 Loomis to Hay, No. 244, 251, and 269, Caracas, February 27, March 11, and April 24, 1899, US/DS/V/IL.

12 Andres Vigas, *Perfiles parlementarias* (Caracas, 1893).

13 Vicente Lecuna, *La revolución de Queipa* (Caracas, 1954), pp. 42, 51, 58–75. Barnes reported as commentary on the 1897 election that the polls were dominated by machete-carrying countrymen to prevent the election of Hernández (p. 480).

14 Pedro García Gil, *Cuarenta y cinco años de uniforme. Memorias, 1901 a 1945* (Caracas, 1947), p. 24.

[15] Fernando González, *Mi Compadre* (Barcelona, 1934), p. 66.

[16] Santiago Briceño Ayestarán, *Memorias de su vida militar y política* . . . (Caracas, 1948), pp. 49–65, 107, 124–126, 131, 138, 172.

[17] Gallegos, p. 14.

CHAPTER 6 :

[1] *Novísima recopilación*, lib. VI, tit⁰ 6, ley 1ª.

[2] Eduardo Arcila Farías, *Economía colonial de Venezuela* (Mexico, 1946), p. 171.

[3] Rafael Maria Baralt and Ramón Díaz, *Resumen de la historia de Venezuela desde,* . . . *1797 hasta, 1830* (Bruges and Paris, 1939), I, 37.

[4] "Milicia," in *Enciclopedia universal europeo-americano*, XXXV, 273; Romuald Brunet, *Histoire militaire de l'Espagne* (Paris, 1886), p. 207.

[5] *Novísima recopilación*, lib. VI, tit⁰ 6, ley 7ª; Lyle N. McAlister, "The Reorganization of the Army of New Spain," *Hispanic American Historical Review*, XXXIII, No. 1 (February 1953), pp. 8–9.

[6] *Reglamento para las milicias disciplinadas de infantería y dragones del Nuevo Reyno de Granada y provincias agregadas a este virreynato* (Madrid, 1794); Hector García Chuecos, *Relatos y comentarios* (Caracas, 1957), p. 101. Social friction over incompatibility of rank and of civil occupation is reviewed in Lautaro García, *Miranda* (Caracas, 1957), pp. 68–76.

[7] *Reglamento para las milicias disciplinadas.* The right to other types of fuero helped determine the category of military fuero assigned an individual or unit. In Barquisimeto in 1767, for example, militia companies enrolling city councilmen and encomenderos with class fuero enjoyed more privileges than other units (*Relaciones geográficas de la gobernación de Venezuela [1767–1768]*, p. 113).

[8] Felix Colón y Larriátegui Ximénez de Embrún, *Juzgados militares de Espana y sus Indias* (Madrid, 1788), II, 585–587.

[9] José Sucre-Reyes, *Le système colonial espagnol dans l'ancien Venezuela* (Paris, 1939), p. 127.

[10] García Chuecos, *Siglo dieciocho, Venezolano* (Caracas and Madrid, n.d.), pp. 136–137. The Seven Years War undoubtedly influenced royal action.

[11] Lautaro García, *Miranda*, pp. 67–68.

[12] Augusto Mijares, "La Patria de los venezolanos en 1750," in *El movimiento emancipador de hispano-américana*, II, 259–260.

[13] Magnus Mörner, "Caudillos y militares en la evolucion hispano-americana," *Journal of Inter-American Studies*, II (July, 1960), 296.

14 García Chuecos, *Siglo dieciocho*, pp. 164–166, and his *Relatos y comentarios*, p. 25; Sucre-Reyes, pp. 126–129.

15 Feliciano Montenegro y Colón, *Historia de Venezuela* (Caracas, 1960), I, 160–161.

16 Sucre-Reyes, pp. 129–135; García Chuecos, *Relatos y comentarios*, pp. 99–101.

17 François Raymond Joseph de Pons, *Voyage à de partie oriental de la Terre-Firme dans l'Amérique méridional fait dans les années 1801, 1802, 1803, et 1804* (Paris 1806), II, 79–89; Sucre-Reyes, p. 128.

18 *Real declaración sobre puntos esenciales de la ordenanza de milicias provinciales de España que interin se regla la formal que corresponde á estos cuerpos, se debe observar como tal en todas sus partes.*

19 Juan Vicente González, "Biografía de Martín Tovar" (pp. 25–86), and "Biografía de José Felix Ribas" (pp. 87–282), *Pensamiento político venezolano del siglo XIX* (Caracas, 1961), II, 82, 97.

20 Páez had organized a battalion of civic militia in Caracas, but dispute over its control led to its virtual abandonment. Marginal notes on the letters of Páez by Soublette and Santander clarify the problem and state the decisions of higher authority which would enable Páez to restore under his control the disciplined militia. (Páez to Secretary of War, Caracas, November 4, 1823 and December 13, 1823, in *Archivo del General José Antonio Páez* [Bogotá, 1939–1957], II, 247–248, 301.)

21 Santander to Senate and House, Bogotá, January 2, 1825, in *Cartas y mensajes*, V, 7–19, esp. pp. 17–18; Santander to President of House, January 31, 1825, *Cartas*, 140; Santander to President of Senate, January 11, 1825, *Cartas*, 397–400.

22 *Acuerdos del consejo de gobierno de la República de Colombia, 1821–1827* (Bogotá, 1940), I, 253, and II, 67; Restrepo, *Diario Político Militar . . .* (Bogotá, 1954), I, 263.

23 Santander to President of Senate, January 5, 1826, *Cartas y mensajes*, VI, pp. 24–27.

24 *El Colombiano*, No. 160, June 7, 1826.

25 *Gaceta del Gobierno*, No. 9, October 13, 1827, gives the militia law an April 1, 1826 date.

26 *Gaceta del Gobierno*, July 25, 1829.

27 See above, pp. 49–50; Diego B. Urbaneja, Minister of Justice and Interior of the Republic of Colombia, to Secretaries of the Sovereign Congress of Cúcuta, Rosario, July 21, 1821, in Archivo del Congreso. Senado. V, Correspondencia oficial, 1820–1821, fol. 196. Urbaneja commented on the "continual friction between those bodies [cabildos] and Command-

ing General Governors." He hoped that a clear delineation of functions between civil and military officials would end the friction. For an example of the problem see Gabriel Valera, Civil Governor of Mérida, to Bolívar, Mérida, April 2, 1821, in *Acotaciones Bolivarianas,* pp. 154–155. Such friction was also an important element in the Valencia insurrection or Cosiata of 1826 which contributed markedly to the disintegration of Colombia.

[28] Baralt and Díaz, II, 287, 386–387. Governor Fernando Peñalver of the Province of Carabobo may have provided some of the data for Baralt and Díaz. His report to the Secretary of Interior (Trujillo, September 15, 1826) stated that "civil jurisdiction is reduced to nullity because all the militias, active and passive, have been declared under fuero, and the civil authorities are alerted to the fact that in no way may they be opposed to the orders of military authorities" (*Cartas y mensajes,* VI, 459–460, footnote).

[29] Law of October 2, 1830, *Cuerpo de leyes,* pp. 37–46.

[30] Tosta García, *Costumbres caraqueñas,* I, 12–13.

[31] Law of October 2, 1830, *Cuerpo de leyes,* pp. 37–46.

[32] Resolution of October 14, 1830, *ibid.,* p. 83.

[33] Law of May 14, 1836, *Cuerpo de leyes,* pp. 221–223. Legislation was not enough, of course. There was a large disinterest in the population which countered all the politician's assumptions of the loyal citizens gladly cooperating in the general welfare. Local officials, but not citizens, had copies of the militia law, but many citizens and some officials were illiterate. Despite efforts of the national and provincial governments only 66,903 men were listed. There was more likely to be a militia of partisans after the event whose occurrence the existence of a militia was supposed to prevent (Rafael María Baralt, "Lo que es un periódico, *El Correo de Caracas,* No. 4, January 30, 1839, in *Pensamiento político venezolano del siglo XIX,* X, 53, 56). Commentary in *La Bandera Nacional* in 1837 confirmed the last point. It seems that by the time the dust had settled down after the War of the Reforms, some thirty battalions of militia had come into being, which "will tranquillize the fearful and impose silence on those that accuse (the government) of not wanting to fulfill the militia law." (Juan Bautista Calcaño's editorial in *La Bandera Nacional,* No. 1, August 1, 1837, in *Pensamiento político venezolano del siglo XIX,* X, 34.)

[34] Decree of September 25, 1830, *Cuerpo de leyes,* pp. 35–36.

[35] Laws of April 19, 1834, and May 11, 1841, *ibid.,* pp. 195, 487.

[36] Report of the Secretary of War and Navy to Congress of 1844, *Gaceta de Venezuela,* No. 672, February 4, 1844.

[37] Annual report of the Governor of Barinas for 1846, *Gaceta de Venezuela,* No. 827, November 22, 1846.

[38] The Minister of War attributed the problem to the laws of April 24, 1838, on powers of governors and of May 18, 1843, on functions of commandants of arms (*Exposición . . . 1849*, p. 23. For the laws see *Cuerpo de leyes*, pp. 315, 548). Both laws, however, do little more than restate provisions of laws of 1830 (Law of October 14, 1830, on local government, and Decree of September 25, 1830, on commandancies of arms, *Cuerpo de Leyes*, pp. 35–36, 57–63) and as amended in the interval. The friction had its background in the colonial era, and more directly in the quarrel over the reorganized militia in the 1820's which Páez had won as commanding general. As the dominant political figure after 1830, Páez had to share control of the militia with the patriciate, that is, with the local authority, just as he had to accept restoration of the cabildo. In 1860 the Minister of War reported continuing friction, pleaded the greater utility of a professional force, and cited the slowness of militia to enter the field as a major cause for early victories by rebels (*Exposición . . . 1860*, pp. 22–25).

[39] *Exposición . . . 1869*, p. xxxvii.

[40] *Gaceta de Venezuela*, No. 828, November 29, 1846.

[41] *Gaceta de Venezuela*, *loc. cit.*

[42] *Exposición . . . 1845*, pp. 6, 8. Conservative publicist Pedro José Rojas in a speech to the militia of Caracas asserted that the militia was the foundation of the Republic and of political liberty (*Pensamiento político venezolano del siglo XIX*, VII, 184).

[43] *Gaceta de Venezuela*, No. 822, October 18, 1846.

[44] *El General José Tadeo Monágas*, by a member of congress, January 29, 1848, a broadside enclosed in Shields to Buchanan, No. 48, Caracas, January 29, 1848, US/DS/V/IV. The broadside is bound in with Despatch No. 44 of January 7, 1848.

[45] The setup was described as military despotism by Shields to Buchanan, No. 61, Caracas, May 20, 1848, US/DS/V/V. See the *Proclama* of José Antonio Páez, Calabozo, February 4, 1848, which denounced Monágas's tampering with the militia in Serrano, *Violencia*, pp. 63–67.

[46] Wilson to Palmerston, No. 2, Caracas, January 15, 1848, FO/80/54, fol. 12r.

[47] Restrepo, *Diario*, III, 537, 543.

[48] *Exposición . . . 1849*, pp. 30–31.

[49] *Exposición . . . 1854*, p. 21.

[50] *Exposición . . . 1854*, p. 10; *El Patriota*, No. 265, May 6, 1854.

[51] Law of April 24, 1854, *Recopilación*, III, 146–148.

[52] *Exposición* of 1856 (p. 9) and 1857 (p. 16).

[53] *Exposición* of 1883 (p. xi) and 1884 (p. xxviii), and *Memoria* of 1889 (pp. 12–13) and 1897 (pp. 3–5).

[54] *Memoria* of 1898 (p. x), of 1899 (I, v), and of 1903 (p. 6).

[55] For the Military Code of 1882 see *Recopilación*, IX, 493–595, esp. p. 493; Resolution of December 7, 1893, *Recopilación*, XVIII, 173–174; Military Code of 1904, *Recopilación*, XXVII, 477–749, esp. p. 478.

[56] Pedro Manuel Arcaya, *Estudios sobre personas* (Caracas, 1911), p. 195.

[57] Scruggs to Blaine, No. 195, Caracas, March 11, 1891, US/DS/V/XLI.

[58] *Memoria* . . . *1909*, I, ix.

[59] *Exposición* . . . *1860*, pp. 23–24.

[60] Decree of April 8, 1879, *Exposición* . . . *1880*, p. 10.

[61] Rafael Cayama Martínez, *El general Gregorio Segundo Riera. Notas biográficas* (Caracas, 1941), pp. 61–62.

[62] Santiago Briceño Ayestarán, *Memorias de su vida militar y política* (Caracas, 1948), pp. 382–384; Mariano Picón-Salas, *Los días de Cipriano Castro*, 2nd ed. (Barquisimeto, 1955), pp. 15–17.

[63] Middleton to Earl of Derby, Caracas, February 2, 1877, FO/80/247, fol. 90v–91r, 94v.

[64] Briceño Ayestarán, pp. 382–384; Picón-Salas, *Castro*, pp. 15–17.

[65] Picón-Salas, *Castro*, pp. 20–21; Briceño Ayestarán, pp. 21–22; Ramón J. Velásquez's introductory study to General Antonio Paredes, *Como llegó Cipriano Castro al poder*, p. cix.

[66] Resolution of the Minister of Interior, December 7, 1893. *Recopilación*, XVII, 173–174, and Decree of December 21, 1895, *Recopilación*, XVIII, 295–296.

[67] *Mensaje que presenta el General Joaquín Crespo . . . al congreso . . . en 1896*, p. 9.

[68] *Leyes y decretos reglamentarios de los Estados Unidos de Venezuela* (Caracas, 1942–), IX, pp. 349–350.

CHAPTER 7:

[1] Major (r) Marco Tulio Páez, "Liminar," in Garcia Gil, *Cuarenta y cinco años de uniforme* (Caracas, 1947), p. 10.

[2] Radio broadcast by Col. Juan Pablo López Centeno, reproduced in *Revista del Ejército, Marina y Aeronaútico*, XV (June 1938), 21–30, esp. p. 27.

[3] Pp. 295–310.

[4] *Las constituciones provinciales,* pp. 110, 241.

[5] *La constitución federal de Venezuela de 1811,* pp. 197–198.

[6] *Textos oficiales,* I, 205–212.

[7] As quoted in Captain General Emparán's decree of March 22, 1810, in *Gaceta de Caracas,* March 30, 1810.

[8] *Textos oficiales,* I, 222.

[9] *Textos oficiales,* II, 7–10.

[10] *El Patriota de Venezuela,* No. 3, November (?), 1811, in *Testimonios de la época emancipadora,* pp. 385–388.

[11] *Textos oficiales,* II, 35–41; "Bando del supremo poder executivo," July 18, 1811, in *Testimonios de la época emancipadora,* pp. 467–468.

[12] *Textos oficiales,* II, 229–235.

[13] Col. Tomás Pérez Tenreiro, "Cipriano Castro, ensayo de interpretación militar," *Fuerzas Armadas de Venezuela,* No. 158–159 (August-September 1959), pp. 14–22.

[14] Fernando Rivas Vicuña, *Las guerras de Bolívar* (Bogotá, 1934–38), III, 177–178, 222.

[15] Rivas Vicuña, III, 61.

[16] Santander to Manuel del Castillo, Bogotá, October 9, 1820, *Cartas y mensajes,* II, 335–336.

[17] Santander to President of the House, Bogotá, April 19, 1823, *ibid.,* IV, 98–100.

[18] Santander to President of House, Bogotá, March 16, 1825, *ibid.,* V, 201–202; Santander to Montilla, Bogotá, August 9, 1825, *ibid.,* pp. 319–321; Santander to Bolívar, Bogotá, September 6, 1825, *ibid.,* p. 341; Santander to Senate and House, Bogotá, January 2, *ibid.,* VI, 14; Santander to President of Senate, Bogotá, January 24, 1826, *ibid.,* p. 87; Santander to President of Senate, Bogotá, February 15, 1826, *ibid.,* pp. 149–150.

[19] *Ibid.,* pp. 148–150.

[20] Santander to Bolívar, Bogotá, October 6, 1825, *ibid.,* V, 361; Roberto Botero Saldarriaga in his biography *Francisco Antonio Zea* has also noted the difference between the two categories of officers (p. 143).

[21] Feliciano Montenegro y Colón, *Historia de Venezuela* (Caracas, 1960), II, 117, 206; Caraccioli Parra-Pérez, *Mariño y las guerras civiles* (Madrid, 1958–60), I, 212–215; Santander to Captain Eusebio Borrero, Bogotá, March 21, 1821, *Cartas y mensajes,* III, 76–77, stated that only the military had made Colombia. There was, possibly, a certain selectivity in who should have the opportunity for public leadership in the Venezuelan area.

Thus in a letter marked Top Secret (*reservadísimo*) Páez indicated he was finding a variety of reasons for sending officers of color to Bogotá, and that the Secretary of War was then to detail them to duty elsewhere (Páez to Secretary of War, Maracay, November 23, 1823, *Archivo del General José Antonio Páez*, II, 289). Apparently the practice continued because Santander commented, "from the interior I send nothing to Venezuela but soldiers, and moreover from there come generals, chiefs, and officers to be sent to other departments in all the branches of administration" (Santander to Montilla, Bogotá, March 18, 1825, *Cartas y mensajes*, V, 204). Páez's attitude undoubtedly was part of a general reaction to the long racial violence of the war. A Spanish commander, Brigadier Juan Manuel Cajigal, had refused to send troops to aid Captain General Montalvo in Nueva Granada in 1815 "because of the state in which many interior towns find themselves today, there being various bodies of guerrillas in action to destroy the white races, . . ." (Cajigal to Montalvo, Valencia, April 9, 1815, "Documentos inéditos para la historia de Bolívar. El Libertador en Nueva Granada, 1814–1815," *Boletín de la Academia Nacional de la Historia*, XIX [January-March 1936], 80).

22 Pérez Tenreiro, pp. 14–22.

23 The Academy of Mathematics was founded in 1830. It was closed in 1870 and reopened in 1877 (*Exposición* . . . *1878*, p. xxii).

24 Decrees of April 11, 1834, and February 14, 1837, and the law of June 26, 1843, *Cuerpo de leyes*, pp. 132, 278, 573.

25 Santander to Pedro Briceño Méndez, Bogotá, February 9, 1826, *Cartas y mensajes*, VI, 128–130.

26 Santander to Montilla, Bogotá, January 29, 1826, *ibid.*, p. 101. For instances of military misconduct which helped shape the thinking of the patriciate in the early 1820's, see Archivo Nacional de Colombia, Solicitudes, XVI. Thus, José Baes of San Juan de los Morros complained in 1821 that a company of the Bravos del Orinoco destroyed his cornfield and orchard (fol. 58r–59bis); Ramón Espejo of Caracas claimed in 1821 that 4 riding mules, 3 pack mules and 2 slaves had departed his hacienda with the army (fol. 250–250bis); Juan José Rivas Pacheco of Caracas reported September 27, 1821, that troops and government agents had raided his cattle ranch (fol. 561–561bis) and six weeks later he reasserted that unit commanders were still treating ranchers like enemies. He submitted a list of incidents (XVII, fol. 90–91thrice).

27 *El Colombiano*, No. 151, April 5, 1826.

28 *Acuerdos del consejo de gobierno de la República de Colombia, 1821–1827* (Bogotá, 1940), II, 161, 171, 240.

29 Pérez Tenreiro, pp. 14–22.

[30] Jorge Basadre, *Chile, Peru y Bolivia independiente,* 1st ed. (Barcelona-Buenos Aires, 1948), p. 757.

[31] Santander to President of Senate, Bogotá, July 1, 1823, *Cartas y mensajes,* IV, 191–192.

[32] *Acuerdos,* II, 260.

[33] Restrepo, *Diario político y militar* . . . (Bogotá, 1954), II, 43.

[34] Fernando González, *Mi compadre* (Barcelona, 1934), pp. 16–18; Restrepo, *Diario,* II, 63.

[35] Santander to President of Senate, Bogotá, March 29, 1825, *Cartas y mensajes,* V, 228–229.

[36] Francisco González Guinán, *Historia Contemporánea de Venezuela* (Caracas, 1909–25), II, 158.

[37] José Antonio Páez, *Autobiografía* (New York, 1871), II, 84; Rafael Maria Baratt and Ramon Díaz, *Resumen de la historia de Venezuela desde,* . . . *1797 hasta* . . . *1830* (Bruges and Paris, 1939), 11, p. 386; *Cuerpo de leyes,* pp. 30, 52–53.

[38] Ker-Porter to Jane, No. 8, Caracas, January 23, 1833, Ker-Porter Papers, 18/13, pp. 157–175, esp. p. 164.

[39] Parra-Pérez, *Mariño y las guerras civiles* (Madrid, 1958–1960), I, 16–18.

[40] Páez, *Autobiografía,* II, 201.

[41] Parra-Pérez, *Mariño y las guerras civiles,* I, 189.

[42] Parra-Pérez, *Mariño y las guerras civiles,* I, 187–188.

[43] Law of September 14, 1830, and decrees of April 1, 1833, May 2, 1834, and April 14, 1835, *Cuerpo de leyes,* pp. 33–34, 116, 133–134, 167.

[44] *Recopilación,* I, 354–359.

[45] Parra-Pérez, *Mariño y las guerras civiles,* I, 303; Baralt and Díaz, II, 431 ff.

[46] Ker-Porter to My Lord, Caracas, July 14, 1835, FO/80/2, fol. 128.

[47] For contemporary accounts of the origins, course and settlement of the War of the Reforms see Montenegro y Colon, II, 318–375, but esp. pp. 355–356 for the motives alleged by Monágas for his rebellion, and Tomás Lander, "Fragmentos, #9," *Pensamiento político venezolano del siglo XIX,* IV, 334–343. The most recent detailed account is that of Parra-Pérez, *Mariño y las guerras civiles,* I, 297–573.

[48] Hill to My Lord, Trinidad, September 28, 1835, FO/80/1, fol. 190–193.

[49] Williamson to Secretary of State, No. 22, Caracas, October 8, 1836, US/DS/V/I.

50 Williamson to Secretary of State, Nos. 3, 5, and 6, Caracas, July 18, 21, and 29, 1835, US/DS/V/I.

51 Williamson to Secretary of State, No. 7, Caracas, August 19, 1835, US/DS/V/I.

52 Parra-Pérez, *Mariño y las guerras civiles*, II, 45; Páez, *Autobiografía*, II, 316.

53 *Gaceta de Venezuela*, No. 831, December 20, 1846; Páez, *Autobiografía*, II, 201.

54 Baralt and Díaz, II, 441; law of April 19, 1836, *Cuerpo de leyes*, p. 195.

55 Decree of May 1, 1836, *ibid.*, pp. 197–198.

56 Páez, *Autobiografía*, II, 316.

57 *Cuerpo de leyes*, pp. 281–282, 322, 377, 422, 468, 512, 539–540, 584, 599, 652–653, 696, 721, 783, 790.

58 Parra-Pérez, *Mariño y las guerras civiles*, II, 142–150.

59 Hall to Secretary of State, Caracas, March 1, 1842, US/DS/V/II.

60 Dr. Laureano Villanueva, *Vida del valiente cindadano general Ezequiel Zamora* (Caracas, 1898), p. 49.

61 *Gaceta de Venezuela*, No. 671, January 28, 1844, and Nos. 673–675, February 11–25, 1844.

62 *Gaceta de Venezuela*, No. 724, February 25, 1845.

63 *Gaceta de Venezuela*, No. 740, June 1, 1845.

64 Decree of December 14, 1847, in *La Prensa*, No. 81, December 25, 1847.

65 *Cuerpo de leyes*, p. 733.

66 Wilson to Palmerston, Caracas, January 23, 1847, FO/80/45, fol. 47v–48r.

67 Wilson to Palmerston, Caracas, May 13, 1847, FO/80/45, fol. 137 v.

68 *Gaceta extraordinaria de Venezuela*, No. 861, May 28, 1847.

69 *La Prensa*, Nos. 77, 79, 80, November 27 and December 11 and 18, 1847. In July the threat of military despotism had been an exotic plant destroyed in 1836, and the real threat to Venezuela was Antonio Leocadio Guzmán's political demagoguery arrayed in high principles and liberty (No. 56, July 5, 1847). United States Chargé Shields reported commentary that Monágas's policy was like that of Bolívar in Colombia, "moulding the Republic into a military form" (Shields to Buchanan, No. 47, Caracas, January 7, 1848, US/DS/V/IV).

70 *El Jeneral José Tadeo Monágas,* by a member of congress, Caracas, January 29, 1848, broadside enclosure to Shields to Buchanan, No. 48, Caracas, January 29, 1848, US/DS/V/IV.

71 Eames to Cass, No. 47, Caracas, March 23, 1858, *ibid.*, XI.

[72] Former Minister of Foreign Affairs of Venezuela Juan Manrique to United States Chargé Shields, Curaçao, April 29, 1848, *Diplomatic Correspondence of the United States,* XII, 561–563.

[73] Páez, *Autobiografía,* II, 451–452.

[74] *El Patriota,* No. 237, October 12, 1853.

[75] *El Patriota,* No. 241, November 9, 1853.

[76] *El Patriota,* No. 241, November 9, 1853.

[77] Shields to Clayton, No. 84, Caracas, April 21, 1849, US/DS/V/V.

[78] *Mensaje del Presidente . . . al congreso nacional,* Caracas, January 20, 1855, a broadside enclosure to Eames to Marcy, No. 7, February 14, 1855, US/DS/V/X.

[79] *Mensaje del Presidente . . . al congreso nacional . . . 1856,* FO/80/116, fol. 116–117.

[80] *Mensaje del Presidente . . . al congreso nacional,* February 1, 1858, FO/80/128, fol. 69v.

[81] An analysis of the loan, its discounts, and the ten million pesos it cost to repay is in Ramón Díaz Sánchez, *Guzmán, elipse de una ambición de poder* (Caracas, 1953), pp. 485–486.

[82] *Exposición . . . 1869,* pp. xxiii-xxiv. The comment of the Minister of War of 1869 could well be a summary of observations published by Cecilio Acosta in 1868 on the injustices which made Venezuelans of all classes and conditions ashamed not to be a revolutionary ("Ideas de actualidad," *Pensamiento político Venezolano del siglo XIX,* IX, 239–246).

[83] *Exposición . . . 1866,* pp. 70–71. The same source reported seventeen generals-in-chief on the retired list (pp. 66–69).

[84] FO/80/211, fol. 331.

[85] "El ejecutivo a los venezolanos," p. 9, FO/80/248, fol. 62–69.

[86] Pérez Teneiro, pp. 14–22.

[87] *Exposición . . . 1866,* p. 14. The Minister of War shared Briceño's opinion.

[88] Ramón Díaz Sánchez, *Guzmán,* p. 553.

[89] See budget for 1876–1877 in *Recopilación,* VII, 320–458, esp. p. 456.

[90] *Exposición . . . 1869,* p. xliii.

[91] *Exposición . . . 1878,* Table A and pp. ix-x.

[92] *Exposición . . . 1880,* p. 17.

[93] *Exposición . . . 1880,* pp. 11–13; *Exposición* of 1881 (p. vii) and 1882 (p. vii).

[94] *Exposición . . . 1883,* pp. v-vi, xxii.

95 *Exposición* . . . *1883*, p. xii; *Exposición* . . . *1885*, p. 12; *Memoria* of 1897 (pp. v-vi) and 1910 (p. viii).

96 *Exposición* . . . *1884*, pp. xiv, xvii.

97 *Exposición* . . . *1887*, p. 6.

98 *Memoria* . . . *1889*, p. viii.

99 *Mensaje que el Doctor Raimundo Andueza Palacios presenta al congreso nacional en sus sesiones de 1891*, pp. 31–33, enclosure to Scruggs to Blaine, No. 195, Caracas, March 11, 1891, US/DS/V/XLI. Andueza Palacios's reorganization of the army coincided with Seijas's denunciation of the armed forces as a major source of fraud, since the organizations were largely nonexistent, yet large annual and supplementary appropriations had been allotted them for years. Even then, he charged, the exiguous portion of the armed forces in existence were defrauded of part of their rations, left untrained in garrison or assigned on permanent leave status (*El Presidente* as reproduced in *Pensamiento político venezolano del siglo XIX*, XI, 121–122).

100 Scruggs to Blaine, No. 306, Caracas, June 28, 1892, US/DS/V/XLII.

101 Scruggs to Blaine, No. 322, Caracas, August 30, 1892, and telegram of September 3, 1892, US/DS/V/XLII.

102 Scruggs to Blaine, No. 343, Caracas, October 7, 1892, US/DS/V/XLII.

103 *Memoria* . . . *1894*, I, vi; Velásquez, "Antonio Paredes y su tiempo," in Antonio Paredes, *Como llegó Cipriano Castro al poder* (Caracas, 1954), p. cix.

104 *Memoria* . . . *1897*, pp. v-vi.

105 Luis Level de Goda, *Historia contemporanéa de venezuela política y militar (1858–1886)*, (Barcelona, 1893), p. xvi.

106 *Recopilación*, XIV, 308–309.

107 *Memoria* . . . *1894*, I, vi, 5–7.

108 *Memoria* . . . *1894*, I, 17–212.

109 Decree of October 7, 1896, *Memoria* . . . *1897*, pp. 102–204.

110 *Recopilación*, XV, 191, and XVI, 120.

111 Decree of January 30, 1893, in *Memoria* . . . *1894*, I, 5–7.

112 Bartelman to Foster, No. 376, Caracas, January 20, 1893, and Partridge to Gresham, No. 29, Caracas, April 27, 1893, US/DS/V/XLIII.

113 Partridge to Gresham, No. 103, Caracas, November 20, 1893, US/DS/V/XLIV; Hazelton to Gresham, No. 40, Caracas, March 9, 1895, US/DS/V/XLV; *Mensaje del General Joaquín Crespo, Presidente, al congreso nacional en sus sesiones de 1898*, p. 15, enclosure to Thomas to Olney, No. 54, Caracas, February 25, 1896, in US/DS/V/XLVI.

[114] *Mensaje del General Joaquín Crespo* . . . *1896*, p. 9

[115] *Memoria* . . . *1894*, I, vii.

[116] *Memoria* . . . *1897*, pp. xv, 8–11, 50–54. For the regulations of the Artillery School see Decree of May 12, 1896, *Recopilación*, XVIII, 369–371.

[117] *Memoria* . . . *1898*, pp. v-vi.

[118] Lucio Pulido to Bartelman, Caracas, June 6, 1895, enclosure to Bartelman to Secretary of State, No. 68, Caracas, June 8, 1895, US/DS/V/VL. Pulido was implementing Article 5 of the Decree of January 30, 1893, setting up the Grand Military Council, *Memoria* . . . *1894*, I, 5–7.

[119] Bartelman to Secretary of State, No. 68, Caracas, June 8, 1895, US/DS/V/VL.

[120] *Mensaje del General Crespo* . . . , *1897*, p. 24; Resolution of July 27, 1896, *Memoria* . . . *1897*, pp. viii-ix. For the salary scale see *Memoria* . . . *1897*, p. viii. Bolivares were introduced as monetary units in 1879, in Decree of March 31, *Leyes y decretos reglamentarios de los Estados Unidos de Venezuela*, XIV, 511–514.

[121] Loomis to Sherman, No. 75, Caracas, February 9, 1898, US/DS/V/XLVIII; *Mensaje del General Crespo* . . . , *1898*, p. 17.

[122] Loomis to Sherman, No. 112, Caracas, April 3, 1898, US/DS/V/XLVIII.

[123] *Memoria* . . . *1898*, pp. xxvii-xxix.

[124] *Memoria* . . . *1899*, I, xix.

[125] *Mensaje del General Ignacio Andrade* . . . *al congreso de 1899*, pp. 44, 48.

[126] *Memoria* . . . *1904*, pp. 3–4.

[127] *Memoria* . . . *1909*, I, xii.

[128] The Academy opened July 5, 1910 (García-Gil, p. 109).

[129] *Memoria* . . . *1903*, p. 24, and of 1904 (p. xxix) and 1905 (p. xii); Resolution of October 25, 1904, *Recopilación*, XXVII, part 2, 362.

[130] *Memoria* . . . *1905*, p. ix.

[131] *Memoria* . . . *1897*, pp. v-vi; *Memoria* . . . *1907*, I, viii.

[132] *Memoria* . . . *1909*, I, ix.

[133] *Memoria* . . . *1910*, p. viii.

[134] Picón-Salas, "Geografía con algunas gentes," *Comprensión*, p. 50.

[135] Picón-Salas, *Castro*, p. 69.

[136] "El doctrinarismo y el progreso," *Pensamiento político venezolano del siglo XIX*, XIII, 187.

BIBLIOGRAPHY

Published documents of a private and official character, biographies, histories, learned and professional journals, and short runs of some nineteenth-century newspapers have provided the major part of the materials used in this study. Nevertheless, very important contributions were made by the ministers of the governments of the United States and of Great Britain near the government of Venezuela. State Department despatches were consulted at the National Archives in Washington, D.C., although some were used in printed form as encountered in the volumes edited by William Ray Manning and in *House Executive Documents*. Despatches of the British ministers to the Foreign Office were available on microfilm at the Bancroft Library of the University of California, as were the private papers of Sir Robert Ker-Porter whose originals are the property of the Fundación John Boulton of Caracas, Venezuela. Incidental use was made of the Archivo General de Indias, Audiencía de Santafé, Legajos 582 and 628; of the Archivo Nacional de Colombia, Salón de la República, Solicitudes, XVI and XVII; and of the Archivo del Congreso de Colombia, Senado, V, Correspondencia oficial, 1820–1821. A heavy debt is acknowledged to the Academia Nacional de la Historia of Venezuela whose publications celebrating the sesquicentennial of independence have been most useful. Unpublished Crown-copyright material in the Public Record Office, London, has been reproduced by permission of the Controller of H. M. Stationery Office.

The bibliography is divided into four sections: Newspapers, Official Documents, Books, and Articles. The category "Articles" will include chapters contributed to symposia whose exclusive concern is not Venezuela. Collections of essays, articles, speeches, and newspaper contributions by the same author will be listed under books. Adequate identification of the archival materials has been given in the preceding paragraph.

I. NEWSPAPERS

El Colombiano, Caracas, 1825–1826.
Gaceta de Caracas, 1808–1812 (Vols. 21 and 22 of Biblioteca de la Academia Nacional de la Historia, Caracas, 1960).
Gaceta del Gobierno, Caracas, 1827–1829.
Gaceta de Venezuela, Caracas, 1844–1847.
El Patriota, Caracas, 1851–1854.
El Patriota de Venezuela, Caracas, 1811–1812 (in *Testimonios de la época emancipadora*, Vol. 37 of Biblioteca de la Academia Nacional de la Historia, Caracas, 1961).
La Prensa, Caracas, 1846–1848.

II. OFFICIAL DOCUMENTS

Acuerdos del consejo de gobierno de la República de Colombia, 1821–1827, ed. Enrique Ortega Ricaurte. 2 vols. Bogotá, 1940.
Andrade, Ignacio. *Mensaje del General Ignacio Andrade, Presidente de Venezuela al Congreso de 1899*. Caracas, 1899.
Andueza Palacios, Raimundo. *Mensaje que el Doctor Raimundo Andueza Palacios presenta al congreso nacional en sus sesiones de 1891*. Caracas, 1891.
Causas de infidencia. Estudio preliminar by Mario Briceño Perozo (Vols. 31 and 32 of Biblioteca de la Academia Nacional de la Historia). 2 vols. Caracas, 1960.
La constitución federal de Venezuela de 1911. Estudio preliminar by Caraccioli Parra-Pérez (Vol. 6 of Biblioteca de la Academia Nacional de la Historia). Caracas, 1959.
Las constituciones provinciales. Estudio preliminar by Angel Francisco Brice (Vol. 7 of Biblioteca de la Academia Nacional de la Historia). Caracas, 1959.
Crespo, Joaquín. *Mensaje del General Joaquín Crespo, Presidente, al congreso nacional en sus sesiones de 1896* [also those for 1897 and 1898]. Caracas, 1896 [1897, 1898].
Cuerpo de leyes de Venezuela con un índice alfabético razonado y referente . . . I, . . . 1830 hasta 1850. . . . Official edition. Caracas, 1851.
Diplomatic Correspondence of the United States: Inter-American Affairs, 1831–1860, ed. William Ray Manning. 12 vols. Washington, D.C., 1932–1939.
Leyes y decretos reglamentarios de los Estados Unidos de Venezuela. 18 vols. Caracas, 1942–1944.
Libro de actas del supremo congreso de Venezuela, 1811–1812. Estudio preliminar by Ramón Díaz Sánchez (Vols. 3 and 4 of Biblioteca de la Academia Nacional de la Historia). 2 vols. Caracas, 1959.

Memoria que dirige al congreso de los Estados Unidos de Venezuela el ministro de guerra y marina [prior to 1889 the *memoria* was an *exposición*. Title may vary slightly from year to year]. Caracas, 1831–1910.

Monágas, José Gregorio. *Mensaje del presidente José Gregorio Monágas al congreso nacional.* Caracas, January 20, 1855.

Monágas, José Tadeo. *Mensaje del presidente José Tadeo Monágas al congreso nacional en sus sesiones de 1856.* Caracas, 1856.

————. *Mensaje del presidente José Tadeo Monágas al congreso nacional.* Caracas, February 1, 1858.

Novísima recopilación de las leyes de España (Vols. VII-X of *Los códigos españoles concordatos y anotados*). 12 vols. Madrid, 1847–1851.

Real declaración sobre puntos esenciales de la ordenanza de milicias provinciales de España que interin se regla la formal que corresponde a estos cuerpos, se debe observar como tal an todas sus partes. Reprinted in Mexico, 1781.

Recopilación de leyes y decretos de Venezuela. Official edition. 51 vols. Caracas, 1874–1929.

Reglamento para las milicias disciplinadas de infantería y dragones del Nuevo Reyno de Granada y provincias agregadas a este virreynato. Madrid, 1794.

Relaciones geográficas de la gobernación de Venezuela (1767–1768), prologue and notes by Angel de Altolaguirre y Duval. Madrid, 1908.

Testimonios de la época emancipadora. Estudio preliminar by Arturo Uslar Pietri (Vol. 37 of Biblioteca de la Academia Nacional de la Historia). Caracas, 1961.

Textos oficiales de la primera república de Venezuela. Pórtico by Cristóbal L. Mendoza. *Estudio preliminar* by P. Pedro Pablo Barnola, S.J. (Vols. 1 and 2 of Biblioteca de la Academia Nacional de la Historia). 2 vols. Caracas, 1959.

United States Congress. *House Executive Documents.* 39th Congress, 2nd Session; 40th Congress, 2nd and 3rd Sessions; 43rd Congress, 1st Session. Washington, D.C.

III. BOOKS

Academia Nacional de la Historia. Mesa Redonda de la Comisión de Historia del Instituto Panamericano de Geografía e Historia. *El movimiento emancipador de hispanoamérica. Actas y ponencias.* 4 vols. Caracas, 1961.

Acotaciones bolivarianas. Decretos marginales del Libertador (1813–1830), ed. Fundación John Boulton. Caracas, 1960.

Alfonzo, Luis Jerónimo. *Breve análisis del pasado de Venezuela.* Caracas, 1872.

Andara, José Ladislao. *La evolución social y política de Venezuela.* Caracas, 1899.

————. *De política e historia.* Curaçao, 1904.

Arcaya, Pedro Manuel. *Estudios sobre personas y hechos de la historia venezolana.* Caracas, 1911.

Arcila Farías, Eduardo. *Economía colonial de Venezuela.* Mexico, 1946.

Artola, Miguel. *Los orígenes de la España contemporánea*. 2 vols. Madrid, 1959.

Ateneo Científico, Literario y Artístico de Madrid. *Oligarquía y caciquismo como la forma actual de gobierno en España, urgencia y modo de cambiarla*. Madrid, 1902.

Baralt, Rafael María, and Díaz, Ramón. *Resumen de la historia de Venezuela desde el año 1797 hasta el de 1830*, with notes by Vicente Lecuña. *Tiene al fin un breve bosquejo histórico que comprehende los años de 1831 hasta 1837*. 2 vols. Bruges and Paris, 1939 [1st ed. Paris, 1841].

Basadre, Jorge. *Chile, Perú y Bolivia independiente* (Vol. XXV of *Historia de América y de los pueblos americanos*, directed by Antonio Ballesteros y Beretta). 1st ed. Barcelona-Buenos Aires, 1948.

Beneyto Pérez, Juan. *Historia de la administración española e hispanoamericana*. Madrid, 1958.

––––––. *Historia social de España y de Hispanoamérica*. Madrid, 1961.

Blanco Herrero, Miguel. *Política de España en ultramar*. Madrid, 1888.

Bolívar, Simón. *Cartas del Libertador*, ed. Vicente Lecuña and Esther Barret de Nazaris. 10 vols. Caracas, 1929–1930. Vol. XI, ed. Vicente Lecuna, New York, 1948; Vol. XII, comp. and ann. by Manuel Pérez Vila for Fundación John Boulton, Caracas, 1959.

Bolívar Coronado, Rafael. *El llanero (estudio de sociología venezolano)*. Madrid, 1919.

Botero Saldarriaga, Roberto. *Francisco Antonio Zea*. Bogotá, 1945.

Briceño, Manuel. *Los ilustres ó la estafa de los Guzmanes*. Caracas, 195– [1st ed. Bogotá, 1884].

Briceño Ayestarán, Santiago. *Memorias de su vida militar y política; varios lustros de historia tachirense; autbiografia [sic.]; cartas del padre del autor doctor Santiago Briceño y otros documentos*. Caracas, 1948 [i.e. 1949].

Briceño Iragorry, Mario. *Casa León y su tiempo*. 2nd ed. (in his *Obras selectas*, pp. 1–214). Madrid, 1954.

––––––. *Ideario político*. Caracas, 1958.

Brunet, Romuald. *Histoire militaire de l'Espagne*. Paris, 1886.

Carrillo Moreno, José. *Matías Salazar. Historia venezolana*. Caracas, 1954.

Cayama Martínez, Rafael. *El general Gregorio Segundo Riera. Notas biográficas*. Caracas, 1941.

Codazzi, Agustín. *Resumen de la geografía de Venezuela*. Paris, 1844.

Colón de Larriátegui Ximénez Embrún, Felix. *Juzgadas militares de España y sus Indias*. 2 vols. Madrid, 1788.

Croce, Arturo. *Francisco Croce, un general civilista*. Caracas, 1959.

Díaz Sánchez, Ramón. *Guzmán, elipse de una ambición de poder*. Caracas, 1953.

Epistolaria de la primera república. *Estudio preliminar* by the Fundación John Boulton (Vols. 35 and 36 of Biblioteca de la Academia Nacional de la Historia). 2 vols. Caracas, 1960.

Escriche y Martín, Joaquín. *Diccionario razonado de legislación y jurisprudencia*. 3rd ed., corrected and augmented. 3 vols. Madrid, 1847.

Felice Cardot, Carlos. *Antología cabudareña*. Barquisimeto, May 1, 1944.

Finer, Samuel Edward. *The Man on Horseback; the Role of the Military in Politics.* New York, 1962.

Gallegos, Manuel Modesto. *Anales contemporáneos. Memorias del General Manuel Modesto Gallegos, 1925.* Caracas, 1925.

García, Lautaro, S.J., *Francisco de Miranda y el antiguo régimen español* (Vol. 5 of Academia Nacional de la Historia. Mesa Redonda de la Comision de Historia del Instituto Panaméricano de Geografía e Historia). Caracas, 1961.

García Chuecos, Hector. *Historia documental de Venezuela; colección de piezas históricas existentes en el Archivo General de Indias, Sevilla, España.* Caracas, 1957.

————. *Relatos y comentarios sobre temas de historia venezolana.* Caracas, 1957.

————. *Siglo dieciocho venezolano* (Colección Autores Venezolanos of Ediciones EDIME). Caracas and Madrid, n. d. [1956?].

García Gil, Pedro. *Cuarenta y cinco años de uniforme. Memorias, 1901 a 1945,* with "Liminar," by Major (r) Marco Tulio Páez. Caracas, 1947.

Gil Fortoul, José. *Historia constitucional de Venezuela.* 2 vols. Berlin, 1907.

González, Eloy. *Historia de Venezuela.* 3 vols. Caracas, 1943–1944.

González, Fernando. *Mi compadre.* Barcelona, 1934.

González Guinán, Francisco. *Historia contemporánea de Venezuela.* 15 vols. Caracas, 1909–1925.

Grisanti, Angel. *Emparán y el golpe de estado de 1810.* Caracas, 1960.

Hernández Ron, J. M. *Tratado elemental de derecho administrativo. . . .* 2nd ed. 3 vols. Caracas, 1943–1945.

Humboldt, Alexander von, and Bonpland, A. *Viaje a los regiones equinocciales del Nuevo continente hecho en 1799, 1800, 1801, 1803 y 1804 . . . ,* trans. by Lisandro Alvarado. 5 vols. Caracas, 1941–1943.

Lecuña, Vicente. *La revolución de Queipa.* Caracas, 1954.

Level de Goda, Luis. *Historia contemporánea de Venezuela política y militar (1858–1886).* 1 vol. Barcelona, 1893.

Lossada Piñeres, Juan A. *Hombres notables de la revolución del 92 en Venezuela.* 2 vols. Caracas, 1893; Maracaibo, 1895.

McAlister, Lyle N. *The "Fuero Militar" in New Spain, 1764–1800.* Gainesville, 1957.

Magallanes, Manuel Vicente. *Partidos políticos venezolanos.* Caracas, 1959.

Martínez Alcubilla, Marcelo. *Diccionario de la administración española, compilación de la novísima legislación de España peninsular y ultramarina en todos los ramos de administración pública. Comprende la definición de todas las voces de la legislación administrativa; . . .* 4th ed. 8 vols. Madrid, 1886–1888.

Michelena, Tomás. *Reseña biográfica de Santos Michelena. Parte histórica, administrativa y político de Venezuela, desde 1824 a 1848.* 2nd ed. Caracas, 1951.

————. *Resumen de la vida militar y política del ciudadano esclarecido General José Antonio Páez.* Caracas, 1890.

Montenegro y Colón, Feliciano. *Historia de Venezuela. Estudio preliminar* by Alfredo Boulton (Vols. 26 and 27 of Biblioteca de la Academia Nacional de la Historia). 2 vols. Caracas, 1960.

Morantes, Pedro María [Pió Gil]. *Los felicitadores.* Caracas, 1952.
Navarro, Nicolás Eugenio, Msgr. *Anales eclesiásticos venezolanos.* Caracas, 1951.
———. *La iglesia y masonería en Venezuela.* Caracas, 1928.
Notice politique, statistique, commerciale, etc. sur les états unis du Venezuela contenant les renseignements les plus utiles et les plus précis sur ce pays en francais, anglais, espagnol, allemand, & italien et accompagnée d'une carte de la république. Paris, 1889.
O'Leary, Daniel Florencio. *Memorias del general Daniel Florencio O'Leary. Narración.* [A reprint of vols. XXVII, XXVIII, and *Apendice* with some added materials of the *Memorias de O'Leary,* ed. by Simón Bolívar O'Leary. 32 vols. Caracas, 1879–1888.] 3 vols. Caracas, 1952.
Ots Capdequí, José María. *Las instituciones del Nuevo Reino de Granada al tiempo de la independencia.* Madrid, 1958.
———. *Manual de historia del derecho español en las Indias y del derecho propiamente indiano.* Buenos Aires, 1945.
Ovalles, Victor Manuel. *Llaneros auténticos.* (Colección de libros nacionales para el pueblo venezolano of Editorial Bolívar.) Caracas, 1935.
Pachano, Jacinto R. *Biografía del mariscal Juan C. Falcón.* Paris, 1876.
Páez, José Antonio. *Archivo del general José Antonio Páez, documentación del Archivo Nacional de Colombia,* ed. by Enrique Ortega Ricaurte and Ana Rueda Briceño. 2 vols. Bogotá, 1939–1957.
———. *Autobiografía del general José Antonio Páez.* 2nd ed., corrected and augmented. 2 vols. New York, 1871.
Paredes, Antonio. *Como llegó Cipriano Castro al poder. Memorias contemporáneas o bosquejo histórico donde se vé como llegó Cipriano Castro al poder en Venezuela y como se ha sostenido en él. 1906,* with an introductory study, "Antonio Paredes y su tiempo," by Ramón J. Velásquez (pp. vii–cxxii). 2nd ed. Caracas, 1954.
Parra-Pérez, Caracciolo. *Historia de la primera república de Venezuela.* 2 vols. Caracas, 1939.
———. *Mariño y las guerras civiles.* 3 vols. Madrid, 1958–1960.
———. *Mariño y la independencia de Venezuela.* 5 vols. Madrid, 1954–1956.
———. *La monarquía en la Gran Colombia.* Madrid, 1957.
Pensamiento político venezolano del siglo XIX. Textos para su estudio. (Publ. by Presidencia de la República. Ediciones conmemorativas del sesquicentenario de la independencia. Han preparado los textos y redactado las notas Pedro Grases y Manuel Pérez-Vila.) 15 vols. Caracas, 1961.
Picón-Salas, Mariano. *Comprensión de Venezuela* (Colección de Autores Venezolanos of AGUILAR). Madrid, 1955.
———. *Los días de Cipriano Castro (historia venezolana del 1900).* 2nd ed. Barquisimeto, 1955.
Pons, François Raymond Joseph de. *Voyage à la partie oriental de la Terre-Firme dans l'Amérique méridional fait dans les années 1801, 1802, 1803, et 1804.* 3 vols. Paris, 1806.
Pulido Méndez, Manuel Antonio. *Régulo Olivares y su época.* Mexico, 1954.
Restrepo, José Manuel. *Diario político y militar. Memorias sobre los sucesos*

importantes de la época para servir a la historia de la revolución de Colombia y de la Nueva Granada desde 1819 par adelante. (Vols. 1–4 of Biblioteca de la Presidencia de Colombia). 4 vols. Bogotá, 1954. The *indices* of the *Diario* are in Restrepos, *Autobiografía* (Vol. 31 of Biblioteca de la Presidencia de Colombia, Bogotá, 1957).

————. *Historia de la revolución en la República de Colombia.* (Vols. 23, 32, 43, 55, 66, 71, 116, 117 of Biblioteca Popular de Cultura Colombiana.) 8 vols. Bogotá, 1942–1950. This edition was made from the second edition (4 vols., Besançon, 1858) which corrected and enlarged the first edition (10 vols., Paris, 1827).

Riera Aguinagalde, Ildefonso. *Páginas escogidas.* Barquisimeto, 1951.

Rivas Vicuña, Fernando. *Las guerras de Bolívar.* 7 vols. Bogotá, 1934–1938; Santiago de Chile, 1940. Vols. 1–4 are Vols. 49, 51–53 of the Biblioteca de Historia Nacional of the Academia Colombiana de Historia.

Sánchez Espejo, Carlos, Fr. *El patronato en Venezuela.* Caracas, 1953.

Sánchez Viamonte, Carlos. *Historia institucional de Argentina.* (No. 39 of Colección Tierra Firme of Fondo de Cultura Económica). Mexico, 1948.

Santander, Francisco de Paula. *Cartas y mensajes del General Francisco de Paula Santander,* compiled by Roberto Cortázar. 10 vols. Bogotá, 1953–1956.

Sarmiento, Domingo Faustino. *Facundo: civilización y barbarie* (Vol. 20, Colección Hispánica of Doubleday & Co., Inc.). Garden City, 1961.

Serrano, José Aniceto. *Violencia ejercida por el poder ejecutiva de la República de la Venezuela en 1848 contra la cámara de representantes proceder de algunas provincias para salvar las instituciones.* Santo Domingo, 1878.

Siso, Carlos. *La formación del pueblo venezolano. Estudios sociológicos.* New York, 1941.

Sucre-Reyes, José. *Le système colonial espagnol dans l'ancien Venezuela.* Paris, 1939.

Toro, Fermín. *Reflexiones sobre la ley de 10 de abril de 1834 y otras obras* (Colección "Clásicos Venezolanos" of Biblioteca Venezolano de Cultura). Caracas, 1941.

Tosta, Virgilio. *El caudillismo según once autores venezolanos; contribución al estudio del pensamiento sociológico nacional.* Caracas, 1954.

————. *F. Tosta García, militar, político, escritor, académico.* Caracas, 1953.

Tosta García, Francisco. *Costumbres caraqueños. Colección de artículos literarios y políticos, publicados en distintos periódicos y muchos inéditos.* Two vols. in one. Caracas, 1882–1883.

————. *El poder civil. Episodios venezolanos.* 2nd series. Caracas, 1911.

Vagts, Alfred. *A History of Militarism, Civilian and Military.* Rev. ed. New York, 1959.

Vallenilla Lanz, Laureano. *Cesarismo democrático. Estudios sobre las bases sociológicas de la constitución efectiva de Venezuela.* 3rd ed. Caracas, 1952.

Vallenilla Lanz, Laureano. *Disgregación y agregación; ensayo sobre la formación de la nacionalidad venezolana,* 2nd ed. Caracas, 1953.

Vigas, Andres. *Perfiles parlementarias.* Caracas, 1893.

Villanueva, Dr. Laureano. *Vida del valiente ciudadano general Ezequiel Zamora.* Caracas, 1898.

Watters, Mary Chapman. *A History of the Church in Venezuela, 1810–1930,* Chapel Hill, 1933. The briefer Spanish translation by L. Roo, *Telón de fondo de la iglesia colonial de Venezuela* . . . (Caracas, 1951), was also used.

Wise, George Schneiweis. *El caudillo. A Portrait of Antonio Guzmán Blanco.* New York, 1951.

Wolf, Ernesto. *Tratado de derecho constitucional venezolano.* 2 vols. Caracas, 1945.

Yanes, Francisco Javier. *Compendio de la historia de Venezuela desde su des cubrimiento y conquista hasta que se declaró estado independiente.* Caracas, 1944.

————. *Manual político del venezolano. Estudio preliminar* by Ramón Escobar Salom (Vol. 14 of Biblioteca de la Academia Nacional de la Historia). Caracas, 1959.

IV. ARTICLES

Acosta Saignes, Miguel. "Los cofradías coloniales y el folklore," *Cultura universitaria,* No. 47 (Universidad Central, Caracas, January-February, 1955), pp. 79–102.

Alba, Victor. "The Stages of Militarism in Latin America," in *The Role of the Military in Underdeveloped Countries,* ed. John J. Johnson. Princeton University Press, 1962.

Alexander, Robert J. "The Army in Politics," in *Government and Politics in Latin America,* ed. Harold E. Davis. New York, 1958.

Angarita Trujillo, Major Rafael. "Causas y consecuencia de independencia," *Fuerzas Armadas de Venezuela,* No. 163 (Caracas, January 1960), pp. 70–83.

Aramburu, General Pedro Eugenio. "El ejército y la democracia," *Política,* No. 6 (Caracas, February 1960) pp. 35–36.

Arcila Farías, Eduardo. "Integración de la burguesía colonial venezolano," *Política,* No. 8 (April-May 1960), pp. 66–74.

Barnes, James. "A Glimpse of Venezuelan Politics," *The Outlook,* LXXIII (1903), 479–483.

Bosch, Juan. "Masas y sociedad en el año terrible de Venezuela," *Revista Nacional de Cultura,* XXII (Caracas, May-August 1960), 119–127.

Caldera, Rafael. Speech of June 27, 1959, *La Religión,* Caracas, June 28, 1959.

"Los caudillos de Oriente y las elecciones de 1909," *Boletín del Archivo Histórico de Miraflores,* II, No. 7 (July-August 1960), 19–37.

"Documento histórico," *Boletín del Archivo Histórico de Miraflores,* I, No. 6 (Caracas, May-June 1960), 11–16.

"Documentos inéditos para la historia de Bolívar. El Libertador en Nueva Granada, 1814–1815," introd. and notes by Vicente Lecuña, *Boletín de la Academia Nacional de la Historia,* XIX (January-March 1936), pp. 21–112.

Gabaldón Márquez, Joaquín. "El enlace de las generaciones," in *Historia de la historiografía venezolana,* compiled, commented, and indexed by Germán Carrera Damas. Caracas, 1961.

————. "El municipio, raiz de la república," in Academia Nacional de la Historia. . . . *El movimiento emancipador de Hispanoamérica. Actas y ponencias,* II.

Giménez Rodríguez, Lt. Gaudy Eli. "Visión general del bloque a Venezuela, 1902–1903," *Fuerzas Armadas de Venezuela,* No. 163 (January 1960), pp. 60–63.

Humphries, Robin. "Latin America. The Caudillo Tradition," in *Soldiers and Governments. Nine Studies in Civil-Military Relations,* ed. Michael Howard. London, 1957.

Johnson, John J. "The Latin American Military as a Politically Competing Group in Transitional Society," in *The Role of the Military in Underdeveloped Countries,* ed. John J. Johnson. Princeton University Press, 1962.

King, James F. "A Royalist View of the Colored Castes in the Venezuelan War of Independence," *Hispanic American Historical Review,* XXXIII, No. 4 (November 1953), 526–537.

Lieuwen, Edwin. "Militarism and Politics in Latin America," in *The Role of the Military in Underdeveloped Countries,* ed. John J. Johnson. Princeton University Press, 1962.

López Centeño, Col. Juan Pablo. Radio address reproduced in *Revista del Ejército, Marina y Aeronaútico,* XV (Caracas, June 1938), 21–30.

McAlister, Lyle N. "Civil-Military Relations in Latin America," *Journal of Inter-American Studies,* III, No. 3 (July 1961), 341–350.

————. "The Reorganization of the Army of New Spain," *Hispanic American Historical Review,* XXXIII, No. 1 (February 1953), 1–32.

Mayer, John. "El llanero," *The Atlantic Monthly . . . ,* III (1859), 174–188.

Mijares, Augusto, "La patria de los venezolanos en 1750," in Academia Nacional de la Historia. . . . *El movimiento emancipador de Hispanoamerica. Actas y ponencias,* II.

"Milicia," *Enciclopedia universal europeo-americano* (Madrid, 1907–1930), vol. XXXV, 273.

Morán, Lt. Col. Manuel. "Los multitudes y la tropa. Fragmentos del curso de educación moral," *Revista del Ejército, Marina y Aeronaútico,* XIII (Caracas, August 1937), 43–48.

Mörner, Magnus. "Caudillos y militares en la evolución hispanoamericana," *Journal of Inter-American Studies,* II, No. 3 (July 1960), 295–310.

Oropeza, Ambrosio. "El estado constitucional venezolano desde 1830 hasta 1870," *Política,* No. 19 (December 1961), pp. 13–33.

Pérez Tenreiro, Col. Tomás. "Cipriano Castro, ensayo de interpretación militar," *Fuerzas Armadas de Venezuela,* No. 158–159 (August-September 1959), pp. 14–22.

Pierson, William Whatley, "Foreign Influences on Venezuelan Political Thought, 1830–1930," *Hispanic American Historical Review,* XV, No. 1 (February 1934), 3–42.

Pratt, D. C. M. "The Allied Coercion of Venezuela, 1902–1903, a Reassessment," *Inter-American Economic Affairs*, XV, No. 4 (Spring, 1962), 3–28.

Rapoport, David C. "A Comparative Theory of Military and Political Types," in *Changing Patterns of Military Politics*, ed. Samuel P. Huntingdon. Glencoe, Ill., 1962.

Rippy, J. Fred, and Hewitt, Clyde E. "Cipriano Castro, 'Man Without a Country,'" *American Historical Review*, LV, No. 1 (October 1949), 36–53.

Rivas, Angel César. "Orígenes de la independencia de Venezuela," in Instituto Panamericano de Geografía e Historia, *La colonia y la independencia* (Publ. No. 8 of Comisión de Historia, Comité de Orígenes de la Emancipación). Caracas, 1949.

"Servidores de la federación," *Boletín del Archivo Histórico de Miraflores*, I, No. 5 (March-April 1960), 17–21.

Stagg y Caamaño, Federico, "El general Juan José Flores," *Boletín Histórico*, No. 1 (Caracas, December 1962) pp. 9–34.

Stokes, William S. "Violence as a Power Factor in Latin American Politics," *Western Political Quarterly*, V, No. 3 (Summer, 1952), 445–468.

Wychoff, Lt. Col. Theodore. "The Role of the Military in Latin American Politics," *Western Political Quarterly*, XIII, No. 3 (September 1960), 745–763.

INDEX

6
7X = 3

better 2 6
33
58

47X
56Y
6)
67X

13 5
148